D1279382

Careers in Focus

Careers in Focus

PUBLIC SAFETY

THIRD EDITION

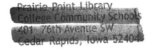

Prairie Point Library
College Community Schools
401 76th Avenue SW
Cedar Rapids, Iowa 52404

Ferguson
An imprint of Infobase Publishing

Careers in Focus: Public Safety, Third Edition

Copyright © 2007 by Infobase Publishing

All rights reserved. No part of this book may be reproduced or utilized in any form or by any means, electronic or mechanical, including photocopying, recording, or by any information storage or retrieval systems, without permission in writing from the publisher. For information contact

Ferguson
An imprint of Infobase Publishing
132 West 31st Street
New York NY 10001

Library of Congress Cataloging-in-Publication Data

Careers in focus. Public safety.—3rd ed.
    p. cm.
    Includes index.
    ISBN-13: 978-0-8160-6594-3
    ISBN-10: 0-8160-6594-2
    1. Criminal justice, Administration of—Vocational guidance—United State— Juvenile literature. [1. Criminal justice, Administration of—Vocational guidance. 2. Law enforcement—Vocational guidance. 3. Vocational guidance.] 1. J.G. Ferguson Publishing Company. II. Title: Public safety.
    HV9950.C35 2007
    363.10023'73—dc22   2007007368

Ferguson books are available at special discounts when purchased in bulk quantities for businesses, associations, institutions, or sales promotions. Please call our Special Sales Department in New York at (212) 967-8800 or (800) 322-8755.

You can find Ferguson on the World Wide Web at http://www.fergpubco.com

Text design by David Strelecky
Cover design by Salvatore Luongo

Printed in the United States of America

MP MSRF 10 9 8 7 6 5 4 3 2 1

This book is printed on acid-free paper.

Table of Contents

Introduction

Nearly every aspect of your life involves policies, regulations, and laws that help to promote public safety. Think about it: The exterior of your house meets certain codes, or rules, so that it won't catch on fire easily. Every time you drive a car, you follow a number of rules so that you won't cause or get in an accident. Even your dog has to obey regulations, like leash laws.

By far, the greatest number of people in public safety—or emergency and protective services—are working at the local level. Almost every community has its own police department. In the smallest communities, a police department may have as few as one or two employees. In larger cities, the members of a police department may be divided into many divisions, each with its own area of the city to patrol. A police force may have specialized divisions, such as a narcotics squad to combat illegal drugs; a vice squad to fight rape, prostitution, and related crimes; a SWAT team that can be called upon in emergency situations; a hostage rescue team; and a bomb squad. Most police departments employ a military-style ranking system. Patrol officers may become detectives. Police officers may rise through the ranks to become sergeants, lieutenants, or even the chief of police for a community. Many other people provide support for a police department, from traffic clerks and police clerks to forensic experts and polygraph examiners.

Other important areas of local law enforcement are probation and parole services. Probation officers are generally attached to the court system, while parole officers work with the correctional system. Both work in cooperation with the police department.

Sheriffs' departments generally operate at the county level, and provide additional law enforcement efforts in many communities in a single county. Almost every state operates its own state police department. They are often called highway patrols because one of their major responsibilities is to ensure the safety of the highways linking communities.

The U.S. Marshals Service, part of the U.S. Department of Justice, is concerned with crimes that cross state lines. Interstate crimes, as they are called, may involve the transport of stolen vehicles and goods from one state to another. U.S. marshals are responsible for tracking down wanted criminals and transporting prisoners. They also operate the Federal Witness Security Program and provide security for federal courts and judges.

Enforcement of federal laws is largely the responsibility of the Federal Bureau of Investigation. The FBI oversees nearly 300 separate violations, including such federal crimes as kidnapping. A principal duty of the FBI is to investigate people and groups that might pose a threat to the internal security of the country. The Central Intelligence Agency is primarily concerned with matters of international security, monitoring world events as they relate to the safety and interests of the United States.

There are many other agencies operating at the federal level, including the Drug Enforcement Agency, the Secret Service, the Customs Service, the Immigration and Naturalization Service, and the Internal Revenue Service. Each agency oversees a particular jurisdiction, or responsibility, of the law. Every agency provides support and cooperation to the others, however, and often works with state and local law enforcement agencies when investigating crimes and apprehending criminals.

The incarceration and rehabilitation of suspected and convicted criminals also occurs at each of the local, state, and federal levels. Communities usually operate jails, which provide temporary housing for people awaiting trial or for convicted criminals awaiting sentencing to permanent prisons. The prison system operates minimum, medium, and maximum security prisons, depending on the nature of the criminal and the crime. Special prisons house mentally ill prisoners or juvenile offenders. People convicted of federal crimes are generally sentenced to prisons operated by the federal government.

Security agencies and detective agencies work to ensure the public safety as well. Many provide bodyguards, security systems, armed security guards, and private investigation services in order to prevent crimes against people and property. Many private companies also work within the correctional system, operating prisons or providing corrections officers or other services. Some private companies also provide police services for universities, airports, communities, and large government facilities and installations.

Careers in emergency and protective services are among the fastest growing in the United States today, according to the U.S. Department of Labor. Increases in crime rates, and especially increases in public anxiety over crime, have led to demands for heightened law enforcement efforts, tougher sentencing laws, and dramatic increases in the security services industry. The attacks on the World Trade Center in New York and the Pentagon in Washington, D.C., in September 2001, have raised concern over domestic security and awareness of the threat of terrorism. Domestic intelligence and investigative operations have increased. The "war on drugs," begun during the

1980s, created a need for larger numbers of law enforcement officials trained and dedicated to reducing levels of drug trafficking. In the mid-1990s, President Clinton passed new tough-on-crime legislation that increased the numbers of police officers employed at the local, state, and federal levels.

The corrections industry has recorded an increase of nearly 80 percent in the number of prisoners in the last decade. The war on drugs has had an especially great impact on the numbers of people being sent to prison. Public outrage at the early release of many violent criminals has led to demands for legislation ensuring these criminals serve the full length of their sentences. More prisons are being built to accommodate them, and more corrections officers are being hired to guard them. At the same time, the overcrowding of many correctional facilities has stimulated pressure for more liberal probation and parole efforts, requiring greater numbers of parole and probation officers.

Immigration and customs officials have seen huge increases in the numbers of people and goods (especially drugs) entering the country illegally. Illegal immigration has become an area of national concern as more and more people have entered the country without the required visas and work permits. Crackdowns on illegal immigration have led to increased numbers of border patrol officers and immigration officials to patrol not only the country's borders, but to seek out illegal immigrants in communities across the United States. Employment of border patrol officers, immigration officials, and customs officials remains largely unaffected by changes in the economy.

Intelligence activities remain an important element of government, despite the ending of the Cold War. The breakup of the Soviet Union has created new political situations and instabilities that must be continually monitored and analyzed for their effect on the interests and security of the United States. Terrorist attacks on U.S. targets overseas and at home continue, and a primary function of the country's intelligence agencies is to identity, intercept, and pursue terrorists who seek to harm the country, its citizens, and its allies.

Private security activities have been stepped up, especially as many U.S. companies have begun to compete in a global economy. Computer technology is a particularly fast-growing area of corporate security, as computers and computer transmissions of information have become more commonplace across a variety of industries.

Each article in this book discusses a particular public safety occupation in detail. The information comes from Ferguson's *Encyclopedia of Careers and Vocational Guidance*, but the articles here have been updated and revised with the latest information from the U.S. Department of Labor and other sources. The following paragraphs detail the sections and features that appear in the book.

The **Quick Facts** section provides a brief summary of the career, including recommended school subjects, personal skills, work environment, minimum educational requirements, salary ranges, certification or licensing requirements, and employment outlook. This section also provides acronyms and identification numbers for the following government classification indexes: the O*NET Dictionary of Occupational Titles (DOT), the Guide to Occupational Exploration (GOE), the National Occupational Classification (NOC) Index, and the Occupational Information Network (O*NET)-Standard Occupational Classification System (SOC) index. The DOT, GOE, and O*NET-SOC indexes have been created by the U.S. government; the NOC index is Canada's career classification system. Readers can use the identification numbers listed in the Quick Facts section to access further information about a career. Print editions of the DOT (O*NET Dictionary of Occupational Titles. Indianapolis, Ind.: JIST Works, 2004) and GOE (The Complete Guide for Occupational Exploration. Indianapolis, Ind.: JIST Works, 1993) are available at libraries. Electronic versions of the NOC (http://www23.hrdc-drhc.gc.ca) and O*NET-SOC (http://online.onetcenter.org) are available on the Internet. When no DOT, GOE, NOC, or O*NET-SOC numbers are present, this means that the U.S. Department of Labor or Human Resources Development Canada have not created a numerical designation for this career. In this instance, you will see the acronym "N/A," or not available.

The **Overview** section is a brief introductory description of the duties and responsibilities of a person in the career. Oftentimes, a career may have a variety of job titles. When this is the case, alternative career titles are presented in this section.

The **History** section describes the history of the particular job as it relates to the overall development of its industry or field.

The **Job** describes the primary and secondary duties of the job requirements, discusses high school and postsecondary education and training requirements, any certification or licensing necessary, and any other personal requirements for success in the job.

Exploring offers suggestions on how to gain some experience in or knowledge of the particular job before making a firm educational and financial commitment. The focus is on what can be done while still in high school (or in the early years of college) to gain a better understanding of the job.

The **Employers** section gives an overview of typical places of employment for the job.

Starting Out discusses the best ways to land that first job, be it through the college placement office, newspaper ads, or personal contact.

The **Advancement** section describes what kind of career path to expect from the job and how to get there.

Earnings lists salary ranges and describes the typical fringe benefits.

The **Work Environment** section describes the typical surroundings and conditions of employment—whether indoors or outdoors, noisy or quiet, social or independent, and so on. Also discussed are typical hours worked, any seasonal fluctuations, and the stresses and strains of the job.

The **Outlook** section summarizes the job in terms of the general economy and industry projections. For the most part, Outlook information is obtained from the Bureau of Labor Statistics and is supplemented by information taken from professional associations. Job growth terms follow those used in the *Occupational Outlook Handbook:* Growth described as "much faster than the average" means an increase of 36 percent or more. Growth described as "faster than the average" means an increase of 21 to 33 percent. Growth described as "about as fast as the average" means an increase of 10 to 20 percent. Growth described as "little change or more slowly than the average" means an increase of 0 to 9 percent. "Decline" means a decrease of 1 percent or more.

Each article ends with **For More Information**, which lists organizations that can provide career information on training, education, internships, scholarships, and job placement.

The revised edition of *Careers in Focus: Public Safety* also includes photos, sidebars, and interviews with professionals in the field.

Airport Security Personnel

OVERVIEW

Airport security personnel is a blanket term describing all workers who protect the safety of passengers and staff in the nation's airports and aircraft. One of the largest group of personnel in this line of work is *security screeners,* who are responsible for identifying dangerous objects or hazardous materials in baggage, cargo, or on traveling passengers and preventing these objects and their carriers from boarding planes. Also included in this group of workers are *air marshals,* who act as onboard security agents, protecting passengers, pilots, and other airline staff in the case of any emergencies while in the air. More than 43,000 people are employed in airport security.

HISTORY

The use of screening and onboard security personnel is not a recent invention. The presence of guards on airplanes originated in the 1960s as a result of a number of hijackings of U.S. planes flying to and from Cuba. These guards, referred to as Sky Marshals, grew in number during the 1970s and then declined in later years with the lower occurrences of airplane hijackings. Airplane security staffing reached several thousand workers at the peak of this hijacking scare, and then dropped to fewer than 100 workers nationwide during its quietest times.

The 2001 terrorist attacks on the World Trade Center and the Pentagon spurred many changes in the realm of airport security.

QUICK FACTS

School Subjects
Computer science
Government
Mathematics

Personal Skills
Following instructions
Leadership/management

Work Environment
Indoors and outdoors
Primarily multiple locations

Minimum Education Level
Some postsecondary training

Salary Range
$30,000 to $80,000 to
$150,000+

Certification or Licensing
None

Outlook
About as fast as the average

DOT
372

GOE
04.02.02

NOC
6651

O*NET-SOC
33-9032.00

Most notably, a new federal agency was born: The Transportation Security Administration (TSA), responsible for overseeing all security at the nation's airports. This agency made airport and airline security a federal responsibility, and as a result, all airport security personnel became federal employees. This was no small task. Previously, private security firms handled security screening in airports. These firms were inconsistent in their hiring and training methods and paid relatively low wages—resulting in high job-turnover rates and inadequate screening of potentially dangerous objects and materials. With the shift of responsibility into the government's hands, standard training and hiring requirements were put in place. In addition to better screening, hiring, and training methods, the technology for screening bags and passengers has improved, increasing the chances that dangerous cargo and on-person threats can be located and prevented from boarding a plane.

THE JOB

Protecting U.S. skies, airports, and passengers is a huge undertaking that requires many qualified, well-trained individuals in different security roles. The most visible airport security worker is the security screener, also called the *baggage and passenger screener.* These workers use computers, X-ray machines, and handheld scanners to screen bags and their owners passing through airport terminals. In addition to using technology to help them identify dangerous items, they also have to depend on their own eyesight to catch suspicious behavior and read the X-ray screens for signs of danger. These workers must be focused and alert, while also remaining personable and courteous to people being screened. The screening process can take a lot of time during high-volume travel days, and passengers waiting in line may be late for a flight, impatient, or simply rude. For this reason, security screeners must be people-oriented, able to manage crowds, and maintain composure in what can be stressful conditions.

The need for security is not limited to the ground. Air marshals, also called *security agents,* have the demanding job of protecting all airline passengers and staff from onboard threats, such as terrorists, hijackers, bombs, or other weapons. These workers are often covert in their operations, meaning they may be dressed and seated like an average passenger to be able to watch for suspicious behavior and surprise a potential attacker. Much of the details of air marshal jobs are classified to protect national security, such as their exact number and identities, routes, and training procedures. The basic duties of their job, however, are similar to those of a Secret Service agent. They must be attentive to all activity that goes on around them, identify potential threats to security, and deal with dangerous individuals or objects once exposed onboard. The main difference between air marshals and other security agents is they must be trained and able to handle possible warfare in a confined space at 30,000 feet in the air.

Another airport security job of high importance is that of *security director*. These workers, hired by the federal government, are responsible for all security personnel within an airport. They oversee the hiring, training, and work of baggage and passenger screeners, air marshals, and other security guards. In the nation's largest airports, such as JFK in New York City or O'Hare in Chicago, directors are in charge of hundreds of workers. Because of the high level of responsibility held by these workers, security directors often have previous experience in crisis management or law enforcement, from such positions as police chiefs or military officers.

REQUIREMENTS

High School

To work in most airport security jobs, you should have at least a high school diploma. Security screeners can sidestep this educational requirement, however, with previous job experience in security. While in high school, take classes in history and government to familiarize yourself with previous events and political threats that have threatened our national security, such as foreign hijackers and terrorist operations. You should also be comfortable working with computers since most jobs in security involve a great deal of technology. Math classes can be beneficial because as a security worker, you must be analytical and observant to identify and catch dangers before they happen.

Postsecondary Training

All security workers, from screeners to directors, are highly trained before starting their jobs. Screeners are trained on how to operate and identify dangerous objects from the X-ray machines and handheld wands. They also must be prepared to manage potentially dangerous individuals. Screeners currently receive 40 hours of training before their first day at work, and receive an additional 60 hours of training while on the job. This training period may be extended due to increased scrutiny on screeners' performance and heightened national security risks.

Air marshals are rigorously trained in classified training centers across the country, and come to the job with previous on-the-job experience from serving in a military or civilian police force. Similarly, security directors must have previous federal security experience and are trained for up to 400 hours before taking on the responsibility of directing an entire airport security staff.

Other Requirements

All airport security personnel have demanding jobs that require a calm demeanor when under pressure. Screeners often have to stand for hours at a time and assist in lifting passengers' luggage onto the screening belt. Their eyesight must be strong enough to detect even the smallest of possible threats displayed on a computer screen. To ensure that individuals can handle these demands, potential screeners face many physical and vision tests to ensure they are up to the job. All screeners must be U.S. citizens or nationals and pass tests evaluating mental abilities (English reading, writing, and speaking), visual observation (including color perception), hearing, and manual dexterity. Similarly, air marshals and directors of security must pass vision and hearing tests and be in good physical shape to face and dominate potential attackers.

EXPLORING

To explore this job, watch people at work the next time you are at the airport. Notice how many people are involved in screening luggage and passengers. While you should not talk to these screeners and other security staff while they are at work, you may be able to schedule an interview with security personnel while they are on break or perhaps over the phone. Talk to a teacher or your school's guidance counselor for help in arranging this.

You can also learn about security jobs by visiting your local library or going online. Explore the Web sites of the Federal Aviation Administration (FAA) for facts and job descriptions, changes in policy, and even summer camp opportunities. The links at the end of this article are good places to start your research.

EMPLOYERS

In late 2001, airport and airline security was placed under the oversight of the federal government. While private companies may still handle some screening jobs, all security personnel are screened and trained under federal rules and regulations. This shift in responsibility was done to improve standards in security and ensure the safety of U.S. passengers and airline staff. The newly created Transportation Security Administration (TSA) and the FAA are the employers of all airport security staff. There are more than 43,000 people employed in airport security, approximately 28,000 of whom are security screeners working in the nation's airports.

STARTING OUT

Depending on the security level you want to be employed in, you can start out working with no more than a high school diploma and on-the-job training. Security screening jobs are a great way to start out in this line of work. These jobs provide front-line experience in airport security and can offer flexible part-time schedules.

Positions as air marshals or directors of security are not entry-level positions. If you are interested in one of these jobs, you will need previous experience with the police, U.S. military, or other position in which you have gained skills in protecting the lives of others.

ADVANCEMENT

Screening jobs have high turnover rates and, as a result, offer many chances for advancement. After a couple of years of experience in baggage and passenger screening, you can move into higher positions in management or busier traffic responsibility. Security managers may be responsible for hundreds of workers and oversee the hiring and training of new workers.

Positions as air marshals already offer a high level of responsibility, but qualified and talented individuals can advance into manager and director roles, responsible for hundreds and even thousands of workers.

EARNINGS

Before the TSA adopted airline security, screeners were paid minimum wage. But to attract and retain qualified and dedicated workers, earnings have been raised considerably, with most full-time screeners earning salaries of $30,000 to $35,000 a year. Their pay increases as their level of experience and responsibility increases. Air marshals and directors earn much more, with directors topping out at a salary of $150,000 or more—one of the highest salaries in government service.

WORK ENVIRONMENT

As previously stated, any job in airport security is demanding and stressful, especially during high periods of travel, such as the holidays. Screeners face physical challenges of standing, bending, and lifting during their shifts, while having to maintain total visual focus on their X-ray machines or while searching individual passengers by hand.

The job of air marshals can be extremely stressful. These workers must be prepared to overcome an attacker in a confined space without risking harm to any of the plane's passengers. In addition, air marshals must spend considerable time away from home.

OUTLOOK

With the new awareness of airline dangers following recent terrorist attacks, the employment of airport security personnel will grow as fast as the average rate. Despite better pay, security screeners still have high turnover rates due to the high demands involved with the job. This turnover will continue to create many new jobs in the future. While jobs as air marshals and security directors will not be as plentiful, there will always be a critical need for qualified and skilled individuals to protect airplanes and passengers from security threats.

FOR MORE INFORMATION

The FAA offers a wealth of information on its Web site, from airline accident statistics to career guidance. Visit the Education pages for information on summer camps for middle and high school students interested in aviation careers.

Federal Aviation Administration
800 Independence Avenue, SW
Washington, DC 20591-0004
Tel: 866-835-5322
http://www.faa.gov

According to its Web site, the TSA "sets the standard for excellence in transportation security through its people, processes, and technologies." Explore the site for details on the nation's threat advisory level and tips on flying and packing safely.

Transportation Security Administration
TSA-21 Human Resources
601 South 12th Street
Arlington, VA 22202-4220
http://www.tsa.gov

Aviation Safety Inspectors

OVERVIEW

Aviation safety inspectors, who usually specialize in general aviation or commercial aircraft, enforce the regulations of the Federal Aviation Administration. They inspect maintenance, manufacturing, repair, and operations procedures and also certify pilots, flight instructors, flight examiners, repair facilities, and aviation schools. They are responsible for the quality and safety of aircraft equipment and personnel. Aviation safety inspectors are classified under the heading of *transportation inspectors.* There are approximately 26,000 transportation inspectors in the United States.

HISTORY

Although the U.S. Constitution gives Congress the power to regulate and control interstate travel via the highway, railway, and water, it does not mention anything about the air. Indeed, the framers of that document did not foresee the age of air travel that would begin in a little more than 100 years. The Wright brothers may have flown the first airplane in 1903, but air travel was not regulated until 1926, when the Secretary of Commerce was given the authority to create a regulatory system. This system was the precursor to the agencies that would later employ many aviation safety inspectors. The system evolved as much as it could to keep pace with the burgeoning field of air transportation until the 1950s, when it could no longer handle the rapidly occurring changes in the field and became outdated. To address

QUICK FACTS

School Subjects
Mathematics
Physics

Personal Skills
Mechanical/manipulative
Technical/scientific

Work Environment
Indoors and outdoors
Primarily multiple locations

Minimum Education Level
High school diploma

Salary Range
$22,610 to $49,490 to
$91,710

Certification or Licensing
Required for certain
positions

Outlook
About as fast as the average

DOT
168, 196, 621

GOE
05.03.06, 05.04.01, 05.07.02

NOC
2262

O*NET-SOC
53-6051.01

these changes, the Federal Aviation Agency was created in 1958. The Federal Aviation Agency was given the authority to promote the development and safety of air transportation through regulations. One of its responsibilities is to set and enforce safety standards. It later became a part of the Department of Transportation (DOT) and was renamed the Federal Aviation Administration (FAA). Another government agency concerned with aviation safety, the National Transportation Safety Board (NTSB), was established in 1967 as a part of the DOT and was made an independent agency in 1975. The NTSB is responsible for investigating aviation accidents, determining the probable cause of accidents, and making recommendations for safety improvements in the field of aviation. Outside of the United States, the growing need for air safety issues and regulations was addressed by the creation of the International Civil Aviation Organization (ICAO) in 1947, and the International Air Transport Association (IATA) in 1945.

THE JOB

The duties of an aviation safety inspector generally include making sure that aircraft are airworthy, that the facilities and equipment surrounding aircraft are safe, and that the personnel working on or flying aircraft complete their work safely and correctly. The specific duties of aviation safety inspectors depend on the area in which they specialize.

Aviation safety inspectors usually work in one of three general areas: operations, pertaining to the operation of aircraft; manufacturing, pertaining to the manufacture of aircraft or related equipment; or airworthiness, pertaining to the maintenance and repair of aircraft and related equipment in order to ensure safe flight. In addition, the FAA has identified and defined eight different types of aviation safety inspectors: *general aviation avionics inspectors, general aviation maintenance inspectors, general aviation operations inspectors, air carrier avionics inspectors, air carrier maintenance inspectors, air carrier operations inspectors, manufacturing inspectors,* and *cabin safety inspectors.* These inspectors all administer and enforce safety regulations and uphold a set of standards. The differences are in the general areas that the inspectors regulate and/ or the size of the aircraft they inspect.

Aviation safety inspectors working in operations are concerned with the people operating aircraft and their training programs, equipment, and facilities. The inspector evaluates pilots, navigators, and flight instructors and issues initial certification that they are proficient and meet the necessary requirements. This certification is done on a continuing basis, and the inspector is responsible for that as well. They also evaluate the manner in which these workers are trained, the equipment they use, and the facilities in which they work and train, to make sure they meet safety regulations and standards. One way an inspector might do this is by running simulations with flight personnel, ground crews, and air traffic controllers to monitor performance of the people and equipment involved.

Aviation safety inspectors working in manufacturing are concerned with the design and manufacture of aircraft, aircraft parts, and avionics equipment. They examine these materials to make sure they match the necessary design specifications. Inspectors may use hand tools and test instruments to accomplish this. They also issue the original certificates determining airworthiness for all aircraft. Inspectors in this area also inspect manufacturing facilities to make sure they meet safety regulations and standards.

Aviation safety inspectors working in airworthiness are concerned with the repair and maintenance of aircraft, aircraft parts, and avionics equipment. They assess the skills of the mechanics that work on aircraft and related parts and equipment and issue initial certification that they are proficient and meet the necessary requirements. This certification is done on a continuing basis, and the inspector is responsible for that as well. They are also responsible for assessing and certifying repair facilities and evaluating mechanic training programs. Inspectors perform inspections of aircraft to determine airworthiness, checking for any problems due to damage or deficient components. One way they do this is by starting the aircraft being inspected and observing the gauges, meters, and other instruments to ensure they are working properly. These inspectors are also responsible for examining maintenance programs and facilities, the equipment and procedures used for maintenance, and maintenance schedules. They advise whether new equipment needs to be acquired or if existing equipment needs to be fixed or modified. They check maintenance records and flight logs to see if prescribed service and maintenance procedures were performed and completed in a timely manner.

REQUIREMENTS

High School

High school students interested in a career in aviation safety should pursue a college prep curriculum, since a college degree is preferred for many positions in aviation safety inspection. Mathematics and science courses are especially useful. Course work in communications will also be beneficial, because aviation safety inspectors need to ask questions, instruct others, and give oral and written reports of their findings.

Postsecondary Training

A high school diploma or equivalency is the minimum eligibility requirement for all federal aviation safety positions; a college degree may be required for nongovernmental positions. Experience is also required, some of which is general to all aviation safety positions. Other experience is specific to the different positions in the field of aviation safety. A college education can be used to substitute for some or all of the required experience, depending upon each position. For example, the federal government will allow the substitution of one year of school for nine months of general experience. A bachelor's degree in the fields of engineering, aeronautics, or air transportation is especially useful. Mike McKenna, a recent graduate of the Institute of Aviation, University of Illinois-Urbana Champaign who is pursuing a career in aviation safety inspection, adds: "My best advice is do not major solely in an aviation-related field. For example, if you are interested in aviation management, I think it is best to get a basic business degree in addition to your various pilot licenses." McKenna believes that the students who major in engineering while pursuing their pilot's license are "the most marketable after graduation."

All prospective aviation safety inspectors should have general experience that provides them with knowledge of the aviation industry and/or aircraft operation. Examples of positions that would qualify as general experience include being a pilot or crew member, an air traffic controller, an aviation mechanic, or an avionics technician. Internships are also helpful. McKenna says he was "very fortunate to participate in an internship with the National Transportation Safety Board," where his duties included helping investigators throughout the process of determing causes for accidents.

Some positions require specific experience. For example, an aviation safety inspector in operations needs experience as a pilot or copilot, a flight instructor, a flight test pilot, a flight inspector, or an aviation operations inspector. Some positions require that inspectors have the ability to operate specific types of aircraft. This experience can be gained from private flight schools, university flight schools, and military training.

An aviation safety inspector in manufacturing needs experience with quality control in accordance with federal aviation regulations. The quality control experience should be with the production of aircraft, aircraft engines, aircraft propellers, or aircraft assemblies.

Some positions require additional experience in supervision, management, and implementation of quality control programs.

An aviation safety inspector focusing on airworthiness needs experience in supervising the repair and maintenance of aircraft, aircraft engines, or aircraft electronics communications and navigation systems. This experience must include being responsible for following federal aviation standards for airworthiness, or military regulations and safety standards. A job as a field service representative of an aircraft systems manufacturer or an aircraft equipment manufacturer may provide adequate experience for some positions, as well.

Certification and Licensing

Certification requirements vary according to the position. For example, an aviation safety inspector working for the federal government in a position where he or she has to operate aircraft must have a commercial pilot certificate as well as a flight instructor certificate, both with single- and multiengine land and instrument ratings. An aviation safety inspector in a position where he or she has to operate aircraft in the air carrier field must have an airline transport pilot certificate. A commercial pilot certificate with multiengine land and instrument ratings, and eligibility for an airline transport pilot certificate will also suffice. Aviation safety inspectors in the area of manufacturing, working for the federal government at a GS-9 position or above, need an FAA mechanic certificate, with airframe and power plant ratings. All certificates must be current.

Other Requirements

Aviation safety inspectors must be methodical, have an eye for detail, and be able to accept responsibility. They must be persistent and patient as they perform inspections or follow an investigation to its conclusion. They also must be able to communicate well with others in order to reach a clear analysis of a situation and be able to report this information. Inspectors must be able to write effective reports that convey vast amounts of information and investigative work.

For many careers in aviation safety, United States citizenship is required, as well as the ability to pass a background security check. Some positions have a minimum age requirement.

EXPLORING

If you are interested in this career, you can begin exploring by arranging to shadow an aviation safety inspector at work. Talking with aviation safety inspectors and observing them as they work will give you a sampling of their duties, as well as the type of situations they encounter from day to day. Visits and interviews can be arranged through the FAA. Another option that will help you learn about aviation safety inspectors is to arrange to take a tour of an airport. Many aviation safety inspectors began with jobs such as aircraft pilots, air traffic controllers, and aviation mechanics or repair workers. Visiting an airport and taking a tour will give you a broader understanding of the basis of aviation safety and will enable you to observe how aviation safety issues affect those careers and the public travelers who pass in and out of an airport on a daily basis. Visits can be arranged through most airports and many airlines, although there might be limitations due to security concerns. You should be aware that every branch of the military services offers opportunities for vital experience for these jobs, and many jobs that are closely related.

EMPLOYERS

Most aviation safety inspectors are employed by the federal government, with the majority working for the Department of Transportation, namely the FAA, and the NTSB. Other employers of aviation safety inspectors include consulting firms, insurance companies, and companies that specialize in aviation technology and industry. Some inspectors are self-employed and work as independent consultants. Aviation safety inspectors are classified under the heading of transportation inspectors. There are approximately 26,000 transportation inspectors in the United States.

STARTING OUT

Aviation safety inspectors are generally not hired unless they have experience in the field of aviation, for example, as a pilot or crew member, an air traffic controller, an aviation mechanic, an avionics technician, or a manufacturing position in the aviation industry. A combination of work experience in the field of aviation and education in areas such as air transportation, engineering, or aeronautics will count as sufficient experience in some cases. After gaining the necessary experience, those interested in becoming an aviation safety inspector should apply for a position. One of the largest employers of aviation safety inspectors, the FAA, maintains a national register of qualified applicants. Persons interested in being hired by the FAA as an aviation safety inspector should contact the FAA for an application. Applicants who are deemed qualified and eligible for employment are placed on the national register for a period of one year. They are matched to any available job vacancies that fit their qualifications.

ADVANCEMENT

Aviation safety inspectors who demonstrate superior job skills may be promoted to positions with an increase in salary and greater responsibility. Those who exhibit managerial skills may advance to a supervisory position, such as section or branch chief. Inspectors with strong teaching and training skills may become instructors at the FAA Academy. Aviation safety inspectors who have a recognized level of expertise may opt to work for themselves as independent consultants.

EARNINGS

Transportation inspectors had median annual earnings of $49,490 in 2005, according to the U.S. Department of Labor. Salaries ranged from less than $22,610 to $91,710 or more annually.

Aviation safety inspectors receive typical fringe benefits, which may include medical and dental insurance, life insurance, sick days, paid vacation days, and participation in a 401(k) or similar savings plan. In addition, government employees may receive a pension. Self-employed aviation safety inspectors are responsible for their own insurance and savings needs.

WORK ENVIRONMENT

The work environment of an aviation safety inspector varies, depending on their employment situation. They usually work both indoors and outdoors, depending on the location and subject of the inspection or investigation. Many aviation safety inspectors who work for the government, consulting firms, or who are self-employed spend much time in the field and therefore will travel a great deal. Since they are responsible for inspecting aircraft and aircraft facilities, they will need to travel to the necessary locations in order to perform an inspection. Aviation safety inspectors investigating an accident will need to travel to the accident site. Those working for private companies may not need to travel as much, since many of their job duties will be performed in-house. Aviation safety inspectors need to be able to work independently and as part of a team, since both qualities are warranted in different job situations. A normal work-week for an aviation safety inspector is 40 hours; additional hours may be necessary, however, when an important inspection needs to be completed or an accident investigated, for example.

OUTLOOK

The U.S. Department of Labor predicts employment growth for all transportation inspectors to be as fast as the average for all occupations through 2014. There should be more employment opportunities for aviation safety inspectors as the federal government seeks to improve aviation safety and address security threats.

FOR MORE INFORMATION

For career information, contact
Federal Aviation Administration
800 Independence Avenue, SW
Washington, DC 20591-0004
Tel: 866-835-5322
http://www.faa.gov/careers

——————— INTERVIEW ———————

Theodora Kessaris has been an Aviation Safety Inspector for the FAA for the past five and a half years.

Q. What made you interested in aviation?
A. I've been in love with airplanes most of my life. When I was a kid, we'd always look up at the airplanes flying overhead and identify them: 'Look, that's a Boeing 727. And there's a DC-9.'

Q. How did you get your first job in aviation?
A. I actually drove to JFK Airport, after having a falling-out with a boss at a non-aviation related job. I'd decided that was it: I had to be near airplanes. I stopped at the first airline I came upon, which turned out to be Pan Am. I walked in and got hired as a passenger service agent. That was around 1988.

Q. Where did you go to school?
A. I attended an approved FAA dispatcher training school located in the New York area, where I received the requisite 200-plus hours of training for aircraft certification.

Q. **What are the positives, and biggest challenges, of the job?**

A. There are moments when I'm able to have a positive effect on aviation, and that's very rewarding. The biggest challenge in being an Aviation Safety Inspector, however, is in making airlines uphold a higher level of safety. Flight regulations make some of this work easy. The recommendations I sometimes have to make will cost the airline money, though, and this is when good communications skills come into play. It took me a while to learn how to deliver recommendations in a tactful, yet clear way.

Q. **What advice can you give to students who are interested in aviation?**

A. To be happy working in aviation, you have to have a strong interest in airplanes and the aviation industry. And to be an Aviation Safety Inspector, you must be prepared to commit a lot of time to aviation. It won't take 25 years, necessarily, to get to this position, but it can take anywhere from 10 years or more, depending on where you work.

Bail Bondsmen

QUICK FACTS

School Subjects
Business
Government
Mathematics

Personal Skills
Communication/ideas
Leadership/management

Work Environment
Indoors and outdoors
Primarily multiple locations

Minimum Education Level
Some postsecondary training

Salary Range
$23,630 to $42,340 to
$113,290

Certification or Licensing
Required by certain states

Outlook
About as fast as the average

DOT
186

GOE
04.03.01

NOC
N/A

O*NET-SOC
N/A

OVERVIEW

When someone is arrested for a crime, a *bail bondsman* (also known as a *bail agent* or *bail bonding agent*) pays the bail so that person can go free until it is time for the trial. The bondsman charges a fee of 10 to 15 percent of the total cash bond assigned by the court. If the person doesn't appear for trial, the bondsman must either find the person or hire someone, known as a *bail enforcement agent, fugitive recovery agent,* or *bounty hunter,* to find the person and bring him or her back. Because the work bondsmen do relies on criminal activities, larger cities have the greatest need for bondsmen.

HISTORY

Bail bonding is a long-established tradition of the American legal system. Posting bail to temporarily free someone who is accused of a crime began in colonial times. Colonists lived under the English common law that they brought with them. People who were charged with crimes were released if someone in the community would vouch for them. At first, if the accused person didn't show up for the trial, the person who guaranteed the accused person's appearance had to face the punishment that would have been given to the accused person. Later, this practice changed so that property was used to guarantee the appearance of someone for trial. In that way, if the person failed to appear for trial, the person who promised that the accused would appear only lost property and did not have to face punishment. As crime increased and the need for making sure accused people showed up for court grew, the courts continued to allow the practice of posting bail. In fact, the Eighth Amendment to the U.S. Constitution states: "Excessive bail shall not be required, nor excessive fines imposed, nor cruel and unusual punishments inflicted." Bail bonding today allows jail space to be freed for serious criminals and helps to ensure that everyone is truly "innocent until proven guilty."

THE JOB

Bail bondsmen work to ensure that a person released from jail will appear again in court as ordered. A typical case (although, in reality, every case is unique) a bail bondsman handles may play out like this: It's late at night and the bondsman's office phone rings. A woman on the other end of the line says her son has been arrested and his court date for trial is four months down the road. The judge set her son's bail at $30,000, and she doesn't have that kind of money. She doesn't want her son to sit in jail for four months for something she's sure he didn't do. (The bondsman may have doubts about the arrested person's guilt or innocence, but that's not an issue for the bondsman to decide.) The mother wants the bondsman's help in getting her son out on bail. She offers to pay the bondsman's fee, which at 10 percent of the bail amount would be $3,000, in exchange for the bondsman covering the bail. At that point the bondsman must decide if the son is a good risk—if he doesn't show up for his court date, the bondsman loses the money posted for bail. Before deciding to take the case, the bondsman does research. Using the phone and computers, the bonding agent gathers more information, such as the type of crime the son allegedly committed, any past record he may have, if he works and what his employer says about him, and what other ties he has to the community. After this research, the bondsman may decide to post bond or reject the case. If the bondsman takes the case and posts bond, and the client shows up for his court date, the bondsman gets the posted money back. If the client fails to show up for court, either the bondsman himself goes after the client or the bondsman hires bounty hunters (also known as bail enforcement agents and fugitive recovery agents) to track down the son and bring him back. Depending on the state, the court gives the bondsman from 90 to 180 days to have the defendant back for trial before bail money is forfeited to the court system.

Like insurance agents, bail bondsmen are calculated risk-takers. Every time they decide to post bail for someone, they are taking a financial risk. Most bondsmen have reliability standards that they use to determine whether someone is more likely to show up for court or to run and hide. The bondsman looks into the person's criminal record, employment history, living arrangements, family situation, and community ties. The type of alleged crime also affects whether a person will run. The arrestee's past criminal record and the state's case against him or her is looked into as well. Some bondsmen consider first-time offenders bad risks because those people are often most terrified about going to jail. People who have a history of crime patterns, such as prostitutes and drug users, are also considered bad risks. On the other hand, drug dealers and professional criminals are good risks because these groups of people usually need to stay in the same area and they want to keep the trust of a bondsman so they can rely on him or her later.

To help cut down the risk of someone "jumping bail," the bondsman spends a lot of time monitoring the people for whom bail has been posted. Some even include a stipulation in the agreement for posting bail that the accused person must call in on a regular basis to verify his or her whereabouts. If the accused person isn't calling in on schedule, the bondsman can get a head start on tracking down the client.

For some bondsmen, tracking down bail jumpers is part of their job, and it takes up much of their time. Other bondsmen choose to hire bounty hunters, who capture and return the client to the bondsman for a fee. Sometimes the bondsman will pay the bounty hunter as much as 50 percent of the total bond if the accused person is returned. The bondsman pays this high amount because it's better to lose half the money that has been posted for bail than to lose all the money if the runaway isn't returned. For the bail bondsman who takes tracking into his or her own hands, the search can lead all over the country. The bondsmen call the accused's family, friends, employers, and anyone they can find to try and get a lead that will eventually take them to the bail jumper. They use computer databases to check into records showing credit activity, estates, and death certificates. When the person is located, the bondsman or bounty hunter confronts the individual and brings him or her back. For a potentially dangerous "skip," the bounty hunter and a backup team may have to break down a door with guns drawn, or opt to work with the local sheriff's department in the instance of known violent offenders.

Some bondsmen use firearms to protect themselves from possible harm. The bail bondsman's job is mostly desk work, however, and often the reason a client misses a court date is because he or she has overslept, forgotten about it, or thought it was for a different day and time.

REQUIREMENTS

While the qualifications vary from state to state, the basic requirements for a bail bondsman are to be at least 18 or 21 years of age, have a high school diploma or GED, and have no felony police record.

High School

To prepare for a career as a bail bondsman, consider focusing on computers, accounting, mathematics, government, social studies, and geography. Accounting, computers, and mathematics will prepare you to handle bookkeeping, record keeping, and negotiations concerning bail money. Because you'll be using a computer for tracing bail jumpers, try to spend as much time as you can honing your computer skills.

Postsecondary Training

Some college-level course work in criminal justice and psychology and training in law enforcement techniques are helpful. Many of today's bail bondsmen have college degrees in criminal justice, although that is not a requirement. Depending on your state's regulations, you may need to complete a certain amount of specific prework and pre-licensing education. For example, one of Oklahoma's requirements for those wishing to work as bail bondsmen is to complete 16 hours of education sponsored by the Oklahoma Bondsman Association before they can sit for their licensing exam and begin working.

Certification or Licensing

Some states require would-be bail bondsmen to attain a property and casualty insurance license requiring several hours of class work under the jurisdiction of the State Director of Insurance or State Department of Professional Regulation. Wisconsin, Illinois, Oregon, and Kentucky ban for-profit bail bonding altogether. Other states require you to pass a bail-bond certification exam. Most states that require exams or licensing also require several hours of continuing education classes each year to keep the license current. You will need a gun license if you plan to use a firearm.

Other Requirements

Bail bondsmen need to have people skills that allow them to effectively communicate with the clients and law enforcement officers they contact daily. They must also be able to deal with high levels of stress and tense situations. Bail bondsmen who do not hire bounty hunters must be physically fit in order to be prepared for any violent or challenging situation.

EXPLORING

You can explore this career by becoming familiar with the justice system. For example, ask your high school guidance counselor or government teacher to help you arrange for a visit to the local police department. You can get a tour of the facilities, learn about arrest procedures, and hear from law enforcement professionals. In some cases, you may be able to arrange for a police ride-along to get a taste of what it takes to arrest or confront someone who does not want to cooperate. You can also familiarize yourself with the justice system by sitting in on open-court proceedings. Another option is to give a bail bondsman a call and ask questions. Get on the Web and search under *bail bonding* to see just how many bail bondsmen are out there; check out their Web sites to learn what kinds of services are offered. Finally, try to get a part-time job that allows you to deal face-to-face with other people—anything from a crowd-control team member at a concert to a security assistant at an amusement park. Working for a security office or for the local court system as a background checker is great experience as well.

EMPLOYERS

Bail bondsmen usually work for other bondsmen or own their own small businesses. Many bondsmen join together to form a partnership to share the workload and to pool their resources. Established bondsmen usually hire several young bondsmen to do the background checking and research. Although almost all towns and cities have bail bondsmen at work, most bondsmen are in large towns and cities. The larger the population, the greater the opportunity for crime and the greater the number of crimes committed, which means the greater the need for bail bonds to be posted.

STARTING OUT

You probably won't see as many ads in the newspaper for bondsmen as you do for, say, administrative assistants, but keep an eye on the classifieds anyway—especially in the big city newspapers. If you want a more direct approach, try calling your local police for some recommendations of experienced bondsmen that you can contact to inquire about a job. Before becoming a bondsman, get your feet wet by doing background checks, chasing down leads, and handling paperwork. If work as a bondsman isn't immediately available, start out in related jobs, such as security positions. Quite a number of bail agents also start out in the insurance business, learning such things as risk assessment and how to underwrite bonds.

ADVANCEMENT

A bail bondsman can remain an independent agent, owning his or her own business, or can advance to managerial positions with a managing general agent. In a partnership, a bondsman can advance to become the *supervising bondsman*, assigning work to more inexperienced bondsmen. There are various jobs that relate to the work of bail bondsmen, such as property and casualty insurance agent, detective, and the court system jobs of pretrial release officer, release on recognizance worker, and probation officer.

EARNINGS

Because most bondsmen have their own businesses, earnings vary according to how much time and effort they invest in the

What Every Bondsman Should Know

Talk to anyone who is knowledgeable about bail bonding and bail bondsmen, and many of the following terms of the trade are sure to be heard.

Bail enforcement agent: Commonly known as a bounty hunter, the bail enforcement agent tracks down and arrests a bail skipper.

Collateral: Property that is sometimes given to the bail agent to guarantee payment.

Failure to appear: The defendant doesn't show up for the court date, and the bondsman begins the process for tracking the person down.

Premium: The bail bondsman's fee for posting bail for someone.

Skip: Not only does the defendant not show up, he or she runs and hides from law enforcement officials and the bondsman or the bondsman's bail enforcement agent. These bail "skippers" don't have the odds on their side.

job. Another important factor influencing the earnings of bail bondsmen is the number of their clients who show up for their court dates. According to the National Center for Policy Analysis in Dallas, 95 percent of a bondsman's clients must show up in court for the business to be successful. According to information from the *Occupational Outlook Quarterly,* a Bureau of Labor Statistics publication, bail bondsmen just starting out and working for a firm may have yearly earnings of approximately $25,000. The bails set for many common charges, such as driving under the influence (DUI) and drug possession, are often not extremely high, perhaps ranging from $500 or $600 to $3,000 or $4,000. In these cases a bondsman would earn $50 or $60 to $300 or $400, and because of these low amounts a bondsman must successfully handle quite a few cases a year to make a substantial living. While a specific annual salary range is difficult to determine, it may be helpful to consider earnings for insurance sales agents since bondsmen's work is similar to that of insurance agents and they are often regulated under state departments of insurance. According to the U.S. Department of Labor, the median yearly income for insurance sales agents in 2005 was $42,340. Fifty percent earned between $30,330 and $68,050 that same year, while the lowest 10 percent had earnings of $23,630 or less, and the highest 10 percent had earnings of over $113,290. Earnings also depend on where the bondsman conducts business. Larger cities offer the most opportunity to make money; however, a well-run business in a medium-sized city can also be highly profitable.

Bondsmen working for firms may receive typical benefits such as health insurance and vacation time. Those who run their own businesses must pay for such benefits themselves.

WORK ENVIRONMENT

Bondsmen work out of offices; some do the work from their homes. They are usually located close to the courthouse so the accused can get immediate service. Bondsmen can work alone or as a team with other bondsmen and people who monitor clients and research background information. Bondsmen spend a lot of time doing paperwork; they must keep records detailing all of their actions and contracts with clients.

Bail bondsmen who choose to do their own tracking may also spend time traveling to find bail jumpers. Tracking bail jumpers and bringing them back to court can be dangerous because these people are obviously desperate to remain free and will do whatever it takes to stay that way, including resorting to violence.

Bail bonding is not a nine-to-five job. Because people get arrested at all hours, bondsmen are on call 24 hours a day. If a bail jumper needs to be rounded up, hours are spent in surveillance to determine just the right moment to move in.

Bondsmen are in contact with many different people during the course of a day. They interview friends and relatives of a bail jumper and work with court personnel. Bondsmen use beepers and cellular phones to remain available to clients who may need their services.

OUTLOOK

Opportunities for bail-bonding work are growing as people with criminal justice, law enforcement, and insurance training enter and gain success in the field, thus gaining the public's respect for the necessity of this work. Professional Bail Agents of the United States says the bail bondsman career is a growing field, but the use of personal-recognizance bail has had a negative impact on its growth. (When judges release an accused person on their own personal recognizance, there is no need for bail bond service; however, there is also no guarantee that the person will show up for court.)

Bail bonding is an industry under constant scrutiny by the justice system, primarily because of the authority of the bail bondsman to engage in activities that some law enforcers cannot perform (such as entering homes without a warrant in search of a bail jumper and crossing state lines to apprehend someone) and what is said to be a financial rather than moral interest in bringing criminals back to trial.

FOR MORE INFORMATION

Visit this coalition's Web site for information on bail laws and bounty hunter laws nationwide, state associations, and industry news.

American Bail Coalition
1725 Desales Street, NW, Suite 800
Washington, DC 20036-4410
Tel: 800-375-8390
Email: dnabic@aol.com
http://www.americanbailcoalition.com

For general information about the field and for specific information about working in California, contact

California Bail Agents Association
One Capitol Mall, Suite 320
Sacramento, CA 95814-3228
Tel: 916-446-3038
http://www.cbaa.com

For more information on the work of bail bondsmen and links of interest, visit the PBUS Web site.

Professional Bail Agents of the United States (PBUS)
1301 Pennsylvania Avenue, NW, Suite 925
Washington, DC 20004-1719
Tel: 202-783-4120
Email: info@pbus.com
http://www.pbus.com

Bodyguards

OVERVIEW

Bodyguards, sometimes called *personal protection officers* or *personal security workers*, protect their clients from injury, kidnapping, harassment, or other types of harm. They may guard a politician during a political campaign, a business executive on a worldwide trip, a movie star going to the Academy Awards, or anyone else who wants personal protection. Bodyguards may be employed by a government agency, by a private security firm, or directly by an individual.

Bodyguards work in potentially dangerous situations and must be trained to anticipate and respond to emergencies. They may carry weapons. Bodyguards need to combine the ability to react quickly and expertly in a tense or dangerous situation with the ability to predict, prevent, or avoid many of these situations.

HISTORY

People, especially rich and powerful people, have always needed protection. Whether a CEO visiting an overseas plant or a political candidate on a campaign, people who make important decisions or control large sums of money always had guards whom they could trust by their side.

As security demands became more complex, the role of bodyguard evolved and expanded. No longer was it enough to simply know how to use a gun or to be particularly adept at martial arts. Bodyguards were expected to help devise strategies to avoid problem situations. They used new surveillance techniques, planning strategies, and other tactics to anticipate possible dangerous situations.

QUICK FACTS

School Subjects
Physical education
Psychology

Personal Skills
Following instructions
Helping/teaching

Work Environment
Indoors and outdoors
Primarily multiple locations

Minimum Education Level
Some postsecondary training

Salary Range
$22,330 to $37,413 to $70,000+

Certification or Licensing
Recommended

Outlook
About as fast as the average

DOT
372

GOE
04.03.03

NOC
6651

O*NET-SOC
33-9032.00

A bodyguard opens a car door for the man he is protecting. (*Jim McGuire/Index Stock Imagery*)

In recent times bodyguards have become involved in many different types of situations. Rock stars and movie stars hire bodyguards to protect themselves against being mobbed by overzealous fans and paparazzi. Executives of large corporations are also likely to enlist the aid of a bodyguard to protect against possible kidnapping or other types of harm. Bodyguards often accompany their clients overseas because police in other countries might not be able to provide the type of security the clients feel they need. Bodyguards often drive their clients from place to place while on assignment.

THE JOB

Although a bodyguard's ultimate responsibility is relatively straightforward—to protect a client from danger—there are a wide variety of tasks involved in this assignment. Bodyguards are part personal aide and part police officer. As personal aides, bodyguards help plan and implement schedules; as police officers, they protect their clients at public or private events. They often act in their client's business and publicity interests, as well; stories of camera-snatching bodyguards have become common fodder for the gossip pages.

Bodyguards face possible danger whenever they are on duty. When there was an attempted assassination of President Ronald

Reagan in March 1981, for example, his Secret Service bodyguards quickly shielded the president with their own bodies as gunshots were fired. Bodyguards may have to sacrifice their own security in defense of those they are hired to protect. Of course, bodyguards are not just sitting targets. They are trained to react appropriately in any situation, life-threatening or not. Skilled bodyguards do all they can to minimize danger to those they are protecting, as well as to themselves. As a result of their careful preparation, bodyguards carry out most assignments relatively uneventfully.

By keeping a watchful eye on their clients, bodyguards are able to avoid many possible problems. In most cases, people are not actually out to harm a client but are simply interested in meeting an important person. Bodyguards learn not to overreact to these encounters, and in most cases, a polite warning eliminates any potential problem.

When a client hires a bodyguard for a specific event, the bodyguard will determine how many additional people may be needed to provide adequate protection. The client's schedule and travel arrangements will be coordinated for maximum security and, if the client is appearing at a public event, the bodyguard will become familiar with the location, especially the exits and secured areas, in case the client needs sudden and immediate protection from danger.

Bodyguards often work in tandem with other security people as part of a large security operation. For example, bodyguards may help develop a plan to safeguard a major politician who is giving a speech, while *security guards* develop a plan to safeguard the building where the speech will take place. All security personnel meet to discuss overall arrangements to ensure that specific details are worked out. Typically, one person will coordinate the security operations.

Bodyguards are hired to protect their clients, and activities that infringe on this job must be avoided. At an awards ceremony, for example, a bodyguard must keep an eye on the client and not gawk at celebrities. Bodyguards should not confuse the glamour and excitement of an assignment with self-importance. Indeed, it is the person who can remain calm in the midst of an exciting event and can sense possible danger when all eyes are elsewhere who makes a skillful bodyguard.

REQUIREMENTS

High School

Since bodyguards must be prepared for any possibility, the more skilled and knowledgeable they are in a range of areas, the better the protection they can offer someone. If you are interested in becoming a bodyguard, in high school you should take courses in a variety of subjects, including psychology, English, and especially physical education.

Postsecondary Training
Bodyguards often begin their careers in civilian law enforcement or the military, where they learn the necessary skills of crowd control, use of weapons, and emergency response. Those wanting to become a security professional working for a government agency, such as the U.S. Department of State, will need to complete a bachelor's degree. Generally, bodyguards have some higher education, although a college degree is not always necessary. A well-educated person can often be the most responsive to rapidly changing situations, and, of course, work in crowd psychology, law, and criminal justice can help a bodyguard better understand the demands of the job. On-the-job experience with different types of people in stressful situations is an integral part of the training. Depending on the employer, new hires may also need to complete between several weeks to several months of training covering topics such as criminal law, use of firearms, personal protection techniques, and first aid.

Certification or Licensing
Certification, while not required, will enhance your professional image in the eyes of potential employers. The American Society for Industrial Security administers the certified protection professional program. Applicants must have a certain amount of professional experience and pass a multiple choice exam focusing on seven areas of security management: emergency management, investigations, legal aspects, personnel security, physical security, protection of sensitive information, and security management.

Other Requirements
Since many bodyguards are former police officers, bodyguards generally must be above the minimum age for police officers. This minimum age varies from 18 to 21, depending on the city or state. If a bodyguard comes from the police ranks, he or she must also have passed a thorough physical exam. Many bodyguards also begin their careers as security guards or as other types of security personnel, for which they receive special training. Other bodyguards come from a military background.

Excellent physical fitness is a requirement for a bodyguard. Despite a popular image of bodyguards as big and tough men, and despite the fact that larger men can serve as deterrents, extreme physical strength is not an absolute requirement, and many women have made successful careers as bodyguards. It is much more important that a bodyguard combine intelligence, sensitivity, and bravery with the ability to act quickly and decisively. The ability to blend into a crowd is also helpful.

Many bodyguards receive training in martial arts, and increasingly they are incorporating the study of counterintelligence operations, electronic security devices, and surveillance techniques. Bodyguards often have training in first aid. Many bodyguards are also trained in specialized defensive driving techniques that enable them to maintain better control of a vehicle in emergency situations. However, being a bodyguard is not carte blanche to engage in action-movie heroics. Bodyguards must understand the appropriate use of force, especially since they can be arrested—or sued—for going over the line.

Bodyguards who travel overseas must be well versed in the language and culture of the host country. Good verbal skills are vital, and a bodyguard must be able to communicate directions to people at all times. A bodyguard must also be aware of what to expect in any situation. That is why an understanding of the customs of areas in which they will be working can help the bodyguard perceive unusual events and be alert for possible problems. Similarly, the legal use, registration, and licensing of weapons differs from country to country, and the bodyguard who travels overseas needs to be familiar with the regulations governing weapons in the country in which he or she is working.

Since bodyguards often work with important people and around sensitive information, they may be required to take a lie detector test before they begin work. Background checks of their work and personal histories may also be required. Bodyguards who work for clients on a permanent basis must also exercise discretion and maintain confidentiality. Bodyguards should have a keen eye for detail and be able to spot trouble long before it happens. This ability to anticipate problems is crucial. A good bodyguard should rarely have to stop a kidnapping attempt as it occurs, for example, but should instead try to prevent the attempt from happening, through a combination of careful planning and skilled observation. If action is needed, however, the response must be swift and effective.

Learn More About It

Bohm, Robert M. *Introduction to Criminal Justice.* New York: McGraw-Hill, 2005.

Holder, Philip, and Donna Lee Hawley. *The Executive Protection Professional's Manual.* Woburn, Mass.: Butterworth-Heinemann, 1997.

Mares, Benny. *Executive Protection: A Professional's Guide to Bodyguarding.* Boulder, Colo.: Paladin Press, 1994.

Schmalleger, Frank. *Criminal Justice: A Brief Introduction.* 7th ed. New York: Prentice Hall, 2007.

Sciacca, Frank Jr. *Bodyguard Principles.* West Conshohocken, Penn.: Infinity Publishing, 2006.

Thompson, Leroy. *Bodyguard Manual.* London: Greenhill Books, 2006.

Wade, Leigh. *Careers in Private Security: How to Get Started, How to Get Ahead.* Boulder, Colo.: Paladin Press, 2002.

Weaver, Alf, and Robert Ashton. *The First Rock 'N Roll Bodyguard.* London: Sanctuary Publishing Ltd., 2001.

EXPLORING

Because bodyguards must be mature and highly skilled, it is difficult to obtain real opportunities to explore this career while still in high school. Nevertheless, there are chances to take classes and talk to people to get a feel for the demands of the profession. Classes in criminal justice should give an indication of the challenges involved in protecting people. Talking to a police officer who works part time as a bodyguard is another good way of learning about opportunities in this field. Many police departments hire high school students as police trainees or interns, providing an excellent introduction to careers in security and law enforcement.

Without the requisite skills and experience, it is difficult to get summer work as a bodyguard. It may be possible, however, to work in some other capacity at a security firm that hires bodyguards, and in this way interact with bodyguards and learn more about the day-to-day rewards and challenges of the profession.

EMPLOYERS

Bodyguards can find work with private security firms and government agencies. They can also find work with politicians, rock stars, and other individuals in the public eye who need personal protection.

STARTING OUT

Many people begin a career as a bodyguard on a part-time basis; for example, police officers often take on assignments while off-duty from police work. The reason that most of them start on a part-time basis is that the police training they receive is ideal preparation for work as a bodyguard. In addition to the excellent training a police officer receives, the officer is often in a good spot to receive job offers. Someone looking for a bodyguard may call the local police station and ask if there are officers willing to take on an assignment. Then, as a person acquires greater experience as a bodyguard and more and more people know of the person's skills and availability, additional work becomes available. That person may then work full time as a bodyguard or continue on a part-time basis.

Military service may also provide the background and skills for entry into this field. Many bodyguards enter this career after service in one of the military Special Forces, such as the Green Berets or the Navy SEALs, or after experience in the Military Police. Other bodyguards enter this field through a career with private security companies and often begin training while employed as security guards. Careers with the Secret Service, the Federal Bureau of Investigation, or other government police and intelligence agencies may also provide the necessary background for a career as a bodyguard. In fact, a successful history with one of these respected agencies is among the most attractive factors for potential employers.

ADVANCEMENT

Those who enter the field as part-time bodyguards may soon find full-time work. As bodyguards develop their skills and reputation, private security firms or government agencies may hire them. They may be given additional training in intelligence operations, surveillance techniques, and the use of sophisticated firearms.

Some bodyguards find opportunities as *personal protection and security consultants*. These consultants work for private companies, evaluating personal security operations and recommending changes.

They may begin their own security services companies or advance to supervisory and director's positions within an existing company.

EARNINGS

Many bodyguards begin their careers on a part-time basis and earn between $25 and $50 per hour for routine assignments. These assignments might last several hours. Earnings for full-time bodyguards vary enormously, depending on factors such as the guard's experience, the notoriety or prestige of the client, the type of assignment, and whether the bodyguard is employed directly by the client or through a security agency. Highly dangerous, sensitive, or classified assignments generally pay more highly than do more routine protective assignments. Training in special skills, such as electronic surveillance also brings higher wages. According to findings by the Economic Research Institute, bodyguards just starting out in the field average a salary of approximately $22,330. Those with five years of experience average approximately $27,570 annually, and those with 10 years of experience average approximately $31,400. Depending on for whom the bodyguard works, earnings may be higher than these. For example, Distinguished Domestic Services, a placement agency for domestic professionals, reported on its Web site (http://distinguisheddomestics.com) that personal protection officers can expect a salary range of $40,000 to $70,000 annually. The agency also notes that these security personnel have usually had some type of government training. On its Web site, the Bureau of Diplomatic Security of the U.S. Department of State (http://www.state.gov/m/ds/career) reported a starting salary range for its special agents in security of $37,413 to $51,788 in 2006.

Bodyguards employed by private security firms may receive health and life insurance and other benefits. Benefits vary for those employed by private clients. Bodyguards who work as part of a government agency receive health and life insurance, vacation, holiday, and sick leave pay, and a pension plan. Self-employed bodyguards must provide their own insurance.

WORK ENVIRONMENT

A bodyguard goes wherever the client goes. This means that the job can be physically demanding. Bodyguards must also have the strength and coordination to take actions to protect the client if the situation warrants it. A bodyguard must be able to act swiftly and decisively to thwart any attempt to harm his or her client.

Bodyguards must be willing to risk their own safety to protect their clients. They should be comfortable handling firearms and using physical means of restraining people.

Since bodyguards must accompany their clients at all times, there is no set work schedule. Bodyguards often work highly irregular hours, such as late evenings followed by morning assignments. It is also not unusual to work weekends, since this is when many high-profile clients make public appearances. Travel is a frequent requirement of the job.

OUTLOOK

Opportunities for bodyguards are likely to be strong, as more and more people look for protection from an increasing number of threats such as stalkers, terrorists, and violent demonstrators. In addition, the threat of kidnapping and terrorism is always present for politicians, celebrities, business leaders, and others who enjoy wide recognition, and these individuals will take steps to safeguard themselves and their families by hiring bodyguards. As more and more companies enter the global economy, their business will take their executives to more areas of social and political unrest, and companies will need to increase their efforts for protecting their employees.

Government agencies will continue to hire bodyguards, but much of the growth in employment will take place in the private sector. Many bodyguards will find work with private security companies. Some estimates suggest that employment in private security may nearly double over the next decade.

Those with the most skill and experience will enjoy the best employment prospects. While the majority of bodyguards continue to be men, the increasing use of advanced security technologies will open up more and more opportunities for women.

FOR MORE INFORMATION

For information on security careers and the certified protection professional designation, contact
American Society for Industrial Security
1625 Prince Street
Alexandria, VA 22314-2818
Tel: 703-519-6200
Email: asis@asisonline.org
http://www.asisonline.org

For more information on the Bureau of Diplomatic Security and the U.S. Department of State, visit this agency's Web site.

Bureau of Diplomatic Security
U.S. Department of State
2201 C Street, NW
Washington, DC 20520-0099
Tel: 202-647-4000
http://www.state.gov/m/ds

Your local Secret Service field office or headquarters office can provide more information on becoming a special agent. To learn more about Secret Service work, find career fairs, and get contact information for field offices, visit the agency's Web site.

U.S. Secret Service
245 Murray Drive
Building 410
Washington, DC 20223-0001
Tel: 202-406-5708
http://www.treas.gov/usss

Border Patrol Officers

OVERVIEW

Border patrol officers patrol more than 8,000 miles of border between the United States and Canada and between the United States and Mexico, as well as the coastal areas of the Gulf of Mexico and Florida. It is their duty to enforce laws regulating the entry of aliens and products into the United States. They are employed by the U.S. Citizenship and Immigration Service (USCIS) of the Department of Homeland Security.

HISTORY

As long as civilizations have established borders for their countries, people have guarded those borders and fought over them. All over the world, societies have created rules and regulations for entry into their countries. Some welcome strangers from other lands, but other societies only allow foreigners to live among them briefly before requiring them to leave. The borders between the United States and its northern and southern neighbors have been peacefully maintained almost continuously since the founding of the countries.

However, federal immigration laws make it necessary for border patrol officers to protect the citizens of the United States by patrolling its borders. Their job is to prevent illegal entry at all of the borders and to arrest or deport those who attempt to enter illegally. In recent years, an increase in narcotics trafficking has made the job of the border patrol officer even more challenging. In addition to preventing the entry of aliens, border patrol officers also prevent the entry of illegal substances, and patrol the borders to prevent terrorists from entering the United States.

QUICK FACTS

School Subjects
Foreign language
Geography
Government

Personal Skills
Following instructions
Leadership/management

Work Environment
Indoors and outdoors
Primarily multiple locations

Minimum Education Level
High school diploma

Salary Range
$34,966 to $46,668 to $67,567

Certification or Licensing
None available

Outlook
Faster than the average

DOT
375

GOE
04.03.01

NOC
N/A

O*NET-SOC
N/A

THE JOB

Border patrol officers are federal law enforcement officers. They are hired to enforce the laws that deal with immigration and customs. U.S. immigration law states that people wishing to enter the United States must apply to the government for permission to do so. Those who want to work, study, or vacation in the United States must have appropriate visas. Those who want to move here and stay must apply for citizenship. Customs laws regulate materials, crops, and goods entering the United States. To ensure that foreigners follow these rules, border patrol officers are stationed at every border entry point of the United States.

Members of the border patrol cover the border on foot, on horseback, in cars or jeeps, in motorboats, in airplanes, and, most recently, on mountain bikes. They track people near the borders to detect those who attempt to enter the country illegally. They may question people who live or work near the border to help identify illegal aliens. When border patrol officers find violators of U.S. immigration laws, they are authorized to apprehend and detain the violators. They may deport, or return, illegal aliens to their country, or arrest anyone who is assisting foreigners to enter the country illegally.

Border patrol officers work with local and state law enforcement agencies in discharging their duties. Although the uniformed patrol

U.S. Border Patrol agent John Bryant marches a group of illegal immigrants across a stretch of the Yuha Desert after a Border Patrol helicopter spotted the group hiding in the brush. *(Lenny Ignelzi/AP)*

is directed from Washington, D.C., the patrol must have a good working relationship with officials in all of the border states. Local and state agencies can be very helpful to border patrol officers, primarily because these agencies are aware of the peculiarities of the terrain in their area, and they are familiar with the operating procedures of potential aliens or drug smugglers.

Border patrol officers work 24 hours a day along the borders of Mexico and Canada. During this time, they may be called upon to do "just about anything you can imagine," according to Paul Nordstrom, a GS-7 border patrol agent at Truth or Consequences, New Mexico. "I've worked with snow rescues of illegal aliens, catching attempted murderers, apprehending stolen vehicles," he says. He has escaped gunfire more than once. At night, border patrol officers may use night-vision goggles to spot trespassers. In rugged areas that are difficult to patrol on foot or on horseback, helicopters are used for greater coverage. At regular border-crossing points, officers check all incoming vehicles for people or materials hidden in car trunks or truck compartments.

The prevention of drug smuggling has become a major part of the border patrol officer's work. The increase in drug traffic from Central and South America has led to increased efforts by the USCIS to control the border with Mexico. Drug-sniffing dogs have been added to the patrol's arsenal. Work for border patrol officers has become more dangerous in recent years, and all officers are specially trained in the use of firearms.

Some employees of the USCIS may specialize in areas of immigration or customs. Immigration inspectors enforce laws pertaining to border crossing. They work at airports, seaports, and border crossing points and may question people arriving in the United States by boats, trains, or airplanes. They arrest violators of entry or immigration laws.

Customs officers work to prevent the import of contraband, or illegal merchandise. Most of their work is involved with illegal narcotics. Customs officers search the cargo of ships and airplanes; baggage in cars, trucks, trains, or buses; and mail. They work with travelers as well as with the crews of ships or airplanes. If they discover evidence of drug smuggling or other customs violations, they are responsible for apprehending the offenders.

Occasionally, border patrol officers may also be called upon to help local law enforcement groups in their work. This may involve searching for lost hikers or travelers in rugged wilderness areas of the northern or southern United States.

REQUIREMENTS

High School

The minimum educational requirement for anyone wishing to train as a border patrol officer is a high school diploma, although a bachelor's degree is preferred. If you are still in high school, take geography, social studies, and government courses. This will help give you a general background for the field. Take a foreign language class, specifically, Spanish; fluency in this language will give you an advantage over other job applicants.

Postsecondary Training

College majors in criminal justice, law, and sociology are highly regarded as preparation for this field, as is previous military training or law enforcement experience. Knowledge of Spanish and other languages is also helpful.

Other Requirements

Border patrol officers must be U.S. citizens. Test scores on an entrance exam admit potential patrol officers to the training program. Successful completion of post-academy courses during the one-year probation period following training, as well as acceptable scores on two mandatory tests in Spanish and law, is required before placement. Good character references are important, and civil service tests are also sometimes required.

EXPLORING

Because of the nature of border patrol work, you will not be able to receive direct experience. Courses in immigration law, Spanish, and criminal justice are helpful, however, as is a good sense of direction, geography, and experience hiking in and knowledge of wilderness areas. Also, since the job can be very demanding physically, you should build your stamina and strength by exercising regularly. School and local libraries may have books with information on criminal justice and law enforcement.

EMPLOYERS

The federal government employs border patrol officers. After training and completion of the one-year probation period, a border patrol officer may be appointed to one of four states: California, Texas, Arizona, or New Mexico. These Southwest border states require the most officers, with nearly 150 stations throughout the United States and Puerto Rico. While employment at these sites tends to fluctuate depending on the employers' perception of need for a given area each year, the larger sites employ anywhere from 100 to 1,000 officers, and recent improvements in funding have guaranteed a steady increase for both officers and support staff nationwide.

An officer's placement is determined at the time of graduation. An individual may request relocation at this time, but at the risk of termination. Though not all states are equipped with border patrol stations, all are required to have at least two immigration stations. Upon promotion, supervisory or investigative positions with the USCIS may be available in these areas.

STARTING OUT

Prospective border patrol officers must pass an entrance exam before being accepted into a 16-week training course at one of three Border Patrol Academies: the Federal Law Enforcement Training Center in Glynco, Georgia; the Advanced Training Facility in Artesia, New Mexico; or the Satellite Training Facility in Charleston, South Carolina. The course teaches the basics of the immigration laws the officers will uphold. They undergo physical training and instruction in law enforcement and the safe use of firearms. Border patrol officer trainees are also taught Spanish as part of their training.

After graduation from the Border Patrol Academy, agents return to their duty stations for a one-year probation period, where they will continue their academic and field training under the supervision of a sector training officer. Two mandatory tests in Spanish and law are administered at six and 10 months. All agents must pass these mandatory exams or they will be refused admittance into the border patrol.

Once they complete the course, they will be stationed along the Mexican border. Border patrol officers take orders from their sector chiefs. Border patrol officers generally enter at the GS-5 or GS-7 levels, depending on the level of their education. Entry at the GS-7 level is generally restricted as part of the Outstanding Scholars' Program, which requires a grade-point average of 3.5 or higher during specified periods of an applicant's college career.

ADVANCEMENT

After their first year, all border patrol officers advance to the GS-9 level. From there, they may compete for positions at the journeyman GS-11 level. With experience and training, border

Learn More about It

Andreas, Peter. *Border Games: Policing the U.S.—Mexico Divide.* Ithaca, N.Y.: Cornell University Press, 2001.

Byrd, Bobby, and Susannah Mississippi Byrd, eds. *The Late Great Mexican Border: Reports from a Disappearing Line.* El Paso, Tex.: Cinco Puntos Press, 1996.

Demmer, Byron, et al. *Border Patrol Exam.* 3d ed. Albany, N.Y.: LearningExpress, 2006.

Hart, John M. *Border Crossings: Mexican and Mexican-American Workers.* Wilmington, Del.: Scholarly Resources, 1998.

Lorey, David E. *The U.S.-Mexican Border in the Twentieth Century: A History of Economic and Social Transformation.* Wilmington, Del.: Scholarly Resources, 1999.

Moore, Alvin E. *Border Patrol.* Santa Fe, N. Mex.: Sunstone Press, 1988.

Urrea, Luis Alberto. *By the Lake of Sleeping Children: The Secret Life of the Mexican Border.* New York: Anchor Books, 1996.

Vila, Pablo. *Crossing Borders, Reinforcing Borders: Social Categories, Metaphors, and Narrative Identities on the U.S.-Mexico Frontier.* Austin, Tex.: University of Texas Press, 2000.

patrol officers can advance to other positions. They may become immigration inspectors or examiners, deportation officers, or special agents. Some border patrol officers concentrate on the prevention of drug smuggling. They may advance to become *plainclothes investigators* who spend months or even years cracking a smuggling ring. They may lead criminal investigations into an alien's background, especially if there is suspicion of drug involvement. Others may prefer the immigration area and work checking passports and visas at border crossings. Border patrol officers may also advance to supervisory positions.

With experience, some border patrol officers leave the front lines and work in the service areas of the USCIS. They may interview people who wish to become naturalized citizens or administer examinations or interviews. Many of the higher echelon jobs for border patrol officers require fluency in Spanish. Advancement within the border patrol comes with satisfactory work. To rise to supervisory positions, however, border patrol officers must be able to work competitively. These positions are earned based on the agency's needs as well as on the individual's merit.

EARNINGS

Border patrol officers begin at either the GS-5 or GS-7 grade, depending on their level of education. In 2006, the starting salaries for these grades were $34,966 and $39,797 per year, respectively. GS-9 salaries started at $44,387 per year. The highest nonsupervisory grade for a border patrol officer is the journeyman level, GS-11, which paid between $51,972 and $67,567 in 2006. Officers in certain cities, such as New York, Los Angeles, Boston, San Francisco, Chicago, Washington, D.C., and others are entitled to receive additional locality pay, which adds roughly 16 percent to the base salary. Law enforcement officials employed by the federal government are also entitled to additional pay of 25 percent of their base salary. Overtime and pay differentials for night, weekend, and holiday work can also greatly increase an officer's salary.

As federal workers, border patrol officers enjoy generous benefits, including health and life insurance, pension plans, and paid holidays, sick leave, and vacations.

WORK ENVIRONMENT

The work of a border patrol officer can be tiring and stressful. Because officers must cover the borders continuously, hours are irregular and shifts tend to vary. "Balancing shift work and having to adjust to that in your family is difficult," says border patrol agent Paul Nordstrom. Most officers spend more time outdoors in jeeps, cars, helicopters, or on horseback than they do in offices. Still, there is a great deal of paperwork to process on each person detained, which usually requires several hours. The work may be dangerous, and many decisions must be made quickly. Border patrol officers must confront many people throughout their shift, and they must remain alert for potential illegal entry into the United States. Many people who attempt to enter the United States illegally have undergone extreme risk and hardship. Border patrol officers encounter emotionally intense situations just as frequently as hostile, violent ones. For example, illegal aliens suffer extremes of heat and discomfort of crowding into the back of a hot, stuffy truck in order to enter the United States; returning to their country is oftentimes as uncomfortable. Border patrol officers must be able to cope with the stress and trauma of such situations. Finally, most of those who attempt to enter the country illegally will do so again and again. Even as agents prevent one group from entering the country, elsewhere several other groups of illegal aliens may be successfully crossing the border. Border patrol officers must be able to work at what may, at times, seem a futile and frustrating task.

Despite the difficulty of the job, work as a border patrol officer can be very rewarding. Border patrol officers perform a necessary function and know they are contributing to the safety of our society.

OUTLOOK

The U.S. Department of Labor projects employment for all police officers and detectives (including border patrol officers) to increase faster than average through 2014. There has been growing public support of drug prevention activities, including the prevention of drug smuggling. Public support of the war on drugs has enabled the INS to continue to increase its surveillance of U.S. borders.

After the terrorist attacks in 2001, growing concerns over the level of illegal immigration have created an urgent need for more border patrol officers. The proposed fiscal year 2007 budget requests funding for an additional 1,500 border patrol agents to increase security at U.S. borders.

FOR MORE INFORMATION

For information about employment opportunities, frequently asked questions, and links to other government sites, check out the USCIS Web site or contact

U.S. Citizenship and Immigration Service
425 I Street, NW
Washington, DC 20536-2542
Tel: 800-375-5283
http://www.uscis.gov

Information about entrance requirements, training, and career opportunities for all government jobs can be obtained from the U.S. Office of Personnel Management. For more information about publications, job listings, or qualifying screening exams, contact

U.S. Office of Personnel Management
1900 E Street, NW
Washington, DC 20415-0002
Tel: 202-606-1800
http://www.opm.gov

For current information on employment procedures, compensation, benefits, and requirements, as well as links to helpful books and other sources of information, check out the following Web site:
United States Border Patrol Unofficial Web Site
http://honorfirst.com

═══════════ INTERVIEW ═══════════

William Botts has spent practically his whole life with the INS/ USCIS and the border patrol. After all, his father, Gene Botts, is a 33-year veteran of the Immigration and Naturalization Service who spent 10 years with the border patrol and wrote a book, The Border Game, *on the challenges confronting today's USCIS officers and investigators. William Botts is a GS-13-level assistant border patrol agent-in-charge at the Nogales station. His station is one of eight on the Arizona/Mexico border that comprise the Tucson sector, which is currently the number-one sector for total alien arrests and the number-two sector for narcotics seizures.*

Q. Why did you decide to pursue the border patrol?

A. I was looking for something that was not behind the desk. Unfortunately, in my present position, I still spend more time behind the desk. But I was looking for something outdoors. My father is a 33-year veteran of the INS, a retired investigator, so I had a pretty good idea of the nature of the job. It sounded interesting.

Q. What part of the job do you find most challenging?

A. The smuggling operations. Smuggling organizations, in particular, have grown more sophisticated, with the aid of cellular phones and other means. And narcotics, for the obvious reasons.

Q. Can you recall the first time you were confronted with a dangerous situation?

A. An alien smuggler tried to run me over. This was probably one to one-and-a-half years after I started duty. Now, in particular, it's very dangerous with the increase in narcotics smuggling. There are a lot more aliens, and a lot more guns. We had an agent, assigned to this station, who was killed in the line of duty three days before I arrived at this duty station.

Q. What do you most like about the border patrol?

A. The outdoors. I particularly like this part of the country...And the periodic moments of excitement.

Q. What might others find most challenging about the job?

A. You see a lot of poor people, desperate people. You can certainly understand why they're coming to this country, but our job is to send them back to theirs. It's more than aliens from Mexico. We see Romanians, Bulgarians, aliens from Guatemala, El Salvador, and, more recently, Hondurans and Nicaraguans. You see some really heartbreaking situations.

Q. What is the biggest misconception about the border patrol?

A. The most common misconception is that we have a high degree of dislike for people from Mexico and other aliens, that we treat them poorly. That's just not true. Quite often we are saving the lives of the people we are arresting. We commonly administer first aid to aliens. We carry water and bandages. And we quite frequently feed the people we arrest before we send them back to their country.

Q. What activities can prepare those who wish to enter the border patrol?

A. Physical fitness is chief. A working knowledge of Spanish is also helpful, but not required.

Q. What advice would you give to those wishing to become a border patrol agent?

A. Try to research the job. Contact the border patrol stations. You can ask to speak to an agent or supervisor, or quite often you will be put in contact with a public information officer who can provide you with information. If you live in proximity to a station, just stop by. Also, understand that if you are hired by the border patrol, there is a 99.9 percent chance you will be stationed at the southern border.

Bounty Hunters

OVERVIEW

Bounty hunters, also known as *bail enforcement agents* or *fugitive recovery agents*, track down and return individuals who are fugitives from justice. People who get arrested are often given the opportunity to post bail money so they can go free while waiting for a hearing or trial. When these people post the bail money, they are promising that they will return on the assigned court date. If they do not return on that date, they lose their bail money (or the bail bondsman loses his) and become fugitives from justice. Bounty hunters spend time researching and interviewing to get leads on the person they are tracking. Bounty hunters working in the United States account for thousands of arrests annually.

HISTORY

The history of the bail process dates back to English common law. People who were charged with crimes against the king were allowed to go free if someone else guaranteed that the individual would return. If that did not happen, the person who guaranteed the return of the individual often had to pay the price instead. In America, this process continued but gave birth to the modern bail bondsman and bounty hunter, who worked together to ensure that accused people appeared for hearings, trials, and sentences. Specifically, bounty hunting grew as a profession during the westward expansion of the United States. Because fugitives would often run as far west as possible to get away from local law enforcement, bounty hunters were often found tracking lawbreakers in the Old West. Though in many states fugitive-recovery activities have come

QUICK FACTS

School Subjects
English
Government

Personal Skills
Communication/ideas
Following instructions

Work Environment
Indoors and outdoors
Primarily multiple locations

Minimum Education Level
Some postsecondary training

Salary Range
$20,000 to $40,000 to
$60,000+

Certification or Licensing
Required by certain states

Outlook
About as fast as the average

DOT
N/A

GOE
N/A

NOC
N/A

O*NET-SOC
N/A

to be performed by marshals, sheriffs, and detectives, the bail-bond system ensures that bounty hunters still flourish in our country.

THE JOB

Bounty hunters work in conjunction with bail bondsmen and the court system. The scenario plays out as follows: An individual is arrested for breaking a law. The individual is given the chance to be freed from jail if he or she guarantees to be at court on a certain date by posting a large amount of money. Most people who are arrested do not have these large sums of money on hand, so they enlist the services of a bail bondsman who provides the money to the court. The individual must pay the bondsman a fee—usually 10 percent of the actual posted bond. If the individual does not show up on the court date, the bondsman can either try to bring the person in or hire a bounty hunter to track the person down. The bounty hunter is paid only if the fugitive is returned to court.

After the bounty hunter is on the case, the main goal is to locate the fugitive as quickly and as safely as possible. Although the time frame varies from state to state and court to court, bail enforcement agents usually have 90 days at the most to bring back the fugitive. Locating a fugitive requires research, detection, and law enforcement skills. "Most of the time it takes time and patience," explains bail enforcement agent John Norman. "Many days are spent interviewing people, tracing paper trails, sitting in vehicles for countless hours of surveillance, just to await that moment to re-arrest this individual." Bounty hunters can use almost any means possible to rearrest a fugitive. In most states, they can enter the homes of fugitives if they believe beyond a reasonable doubt that the fugitive is inside. Sometimes the bounty hunter will interview family members or check the trash at the fugitive's home to find a clue as to where he or she has gone. Most bounty hunters use weapons to protect themselves and to persuade a fugitive to return peacefully. "The field can also be very dangerous," Norman cautions. "Getting shot at or knifed is not uncommon." After the fugitive is found, the bounty hunter makes a private arrest of the individual and takes the fugitive back to jail to await trial. "This process of retrieval can be easy sometimes and hard others," Norman adds. Although most bounty hunters rearrest the fugitive themselves, some locate the fugitive and then alert the local law officials to make the actual arrest.

Bounty hunting is not only about tracking people and bringing them back alive, however. Bounty hunting is a business, and like any other business, it must be run efficiently. In order to get work, bail enforcement agents must be able to advertise their services to become part of as many bail bondsmen "networks" as possible. Some bondsmen work with just a select few bounty hunters, while others send out their fugitive recovery requests to large networks of bounty hunters who compete against each other to bring back the fugitive. Because bounty hunters get paid only if they bring the person back, care must be taken to use resources wisely. Someone who spends $1,000 to find a fugitive, with a reward for only $750, will not be in business long. Besides monetary resources, many bail enforcement agents have research assistants who work for them. Enforcement agents must be able to manage their employees in these situations. Bounty hunters also often work under contracts with law enforcement or bail bondsmen. They must be able to draw up contracts and be well-informed regarding all the legal aspects of those contracts.

REQUIREMENTS
High School
Although you will not find a class at school called Bounty Hunting 101, there are some courses that can help you prepare for a job in this field while you are still in high school. Classes in government, political science, communication, and business will help you prepare for the legal and business side of bounty hunting. If you have the opportunity to take self-defense or martial arts courses, they can give you skills sometimes necessary in the actual apprehension of a fugitive. Foreign languages may come in handy as well, depending on the area of the country where you may be working.

Postsecondary Training
You are not required to have any college training to be a bounty hunter. However, training is important for success and safety as a bail enforcement agent. "One way or another, you should have at least some sort of training in law enforcement and criminal justice," John Norman recommends. If a college degree or vocational school is in your future, aim for criminal justice studies or police academy training. If you want to focus immediately on bail enforcement, some training opportunities are available. The National Institute of Bail Enforcement in Illinois and the National Association of Bail Enforcement Agents, for example, provide training seminars. (For contact information on these programs, see the list at the end of this article.)

Certification or Licensing

Regulations covering bounty hunters' activities vary by state. It is, therefore, very important that you check with your state's attorney general's office, department of public safety, or professional licensing board to determine the rules for your area. In addition, it is important to be aware of other state's regulations in case your work takes you there. For example, some states, such as Illinois, prohibit bounty hunting. Some states, such as North Carolina, have as part of their requirements that "bail runners" work for only one bail bondsman or bail bond agency. Other states, such as Mississippi and Connecticut, have licensing requirements for bail enforcement agents; however, the licensing requirements themselves vary from state to state. And finally, some states, such as Georgia, have requirements such as registration with a sheriff's department or other agency. Generally, licensing involves passing a written test, passing a drug test and background check, being at least a certain age, being a U.S. citizen, and having completed some type of approved training. Anyone using a gun must, of course, have a license to do so.

Other Requirements

Bounty hunters must be able to handle high-stress situations that are often dangerous. Because of the nature of the work, the bounty

Bounty Hunters on TV

The Lone Ranger began airing in 1949 and portrayed a ranger and his sidekick Tonto cleaning up the Old West. It helped popularize the Western as a television genre. *Wanted: Dead or Alive*, starring Steve McQueen, aired from 1958 to 1961 and showed bounty hunting as a respectable career. *Gunsmoke* (1955–75) depicted the bounty hunter as lawless instead, and often showed the main character, Matt Dillon (played by James Arness), going up against ruthless bounty hunters. The cameras of *American Bounty Hunter* (1996) and *U.S. Bounty Hunter* (2003) have followed real bounty hunters as they tracked down fugitives. More recently, there have been The Learning Channel's *Secret World of Bounty Hunters* and A&E's reality TV show, *Dog the Bounty Hunter* (http://www.dogthebountyhunter.com). And then, of course, there are always science-fiction treatments of the subject, like the famous 1998 Japanese anime series *Cowboy Bebop*, which follows the misadventures of a group of wisecracking intergalactic bounty hunters.

hunter should be trained in the use of firearms and other weapons. Bounty hunters must be physically fit and able to defend themselves in dangerous situations.

EXPLORING

Bounty hunting can be dangerous, so you may be wondering how you can explore the field without getting hurt. That is a good question, but there are ways you can get an idea about the situations you would be encountering without being thrown into the thick of a fight. First, do some research. Contact your local and state authorities and ask for information about current laws and how they affect bounty hunters. Once you have that information under your belt, you can contact your local police and ask to go on a ride-along with the specific focus on the times officers assist bounty hunters. (This "assistance" is usually just sitting in the patrol car to further persuade the fugitive that this is the real thing.) You may get the chance, from a safe distance, to watch the bounty hunter in action. Some cities and counties also conduct "citizen police academies" that train the public on many police situations and safety issues. Enroll in any programs you can find that provide this kind of information and training. Contact a bail bondsman (you will find many listed in the phone book) and find out if they are also bounty hunters. Ask any questions you may have. Try to interview several bondsmen to get a more balanced view of what it is like to work in the bail bonding and fugitive recovery business. As stated earlier, much of the bounty hunter's time is spent running the business. Join any clubs at school that focus on business, such as Junior Achievement.

EMPLOYERS

Most bounty hunters work independently. Many run their own businesses and contract their services to bail bondsmen and other individuals. Some bounty hunters are also bondsmen, and they combine the services into one business. These bounty hunters are part timers, because most of their time is spent on bail bonding or investigating. "Some [bail enforcement agents] such as myself have their own companies," explains John Norman. "However, a lot of agents work directly under the bondsman. The bondsman is our main source of work in either case." Bondsmen either hire bounty hunters on a case-by-case basis or they hire them as full- or part-time employees. Private individuals also hire bounty hunters for other services, such as recovering missing persons, finding persons who are not paying child support, and uncovering insurance fraud.

STARTING OUT

Although most bail enforcement agents own their own businesses, the majority start out working and learning the business from bail bondsmen or other bail enforcement agents. The best, most direct way to get started in the fugitive recovery field is to approach several bondsmen or bail enforcement agencies in your area. Most bounty hunters start out as *research assistants* or *skip tracers*. Skip tracers do the background and frontline interviewing to try to find the general location of the fugitive. The more training you have, the better chance you will have at landing that first job. You may have to start off in some form of law enforcement before you will be considered experienced or skilled enough to go into bounty hunting for a bondsman. Some starting points include jobs such as security guards, campus police, and researchers for private investigators.

ADVANCEMENT

Because most bail enforcement agents own their own agencies, they are at the top of their business, with no higher position to be had. Because of the competition within the fugitive recovery field, however, there is a drive to be the "best of the best" and have the highest fugitive recovery rate. Bail enforcement agents want to be able to maintain and advertise a very high rate of return, and the best and highest-paid in the field are able to produce over 90 percent of the fugitives they track. Many bail enforcement agents chase the goal of perfection as strongly as they chase each fugitive.

Bounty hunters who work for other bail enforcement agents or bondsmen can work toward owning their own agency. Usually success in tracking down fugitives is the path toward the recognition and marketability necessary to start a new fugitive recovery business.

EARNINGS

The bounty hunting business, like any other, takes time to develop, and bounty hunters who start their own agencies have many out-of-pocket expenses for items such as handcuffs and advertising. Some may end up losing money or only earning enough to break even. For those who manage to build up a business, however, earnings can be quite good. The National Center for Policy Analysis' 2000 report *Privatiz-*

ing Probation and Parole states that bounty hunters generally earn between $20,000 and $30,000 for part-time work. A 2001 article on the CNNMoney Web site (http://money.cnn.com/smbusiness, "Getting Started: Bounty Hunters") notes that while most bonds are fairly small (meaning that a bounty hunter does not earn much from one recovery), annual incomes can be good because there are plenty of fugitives on the run and lots of work is available. According to CNNMoney, bounty hunters generally earn between $40,000 and $60,000 per year. It is important to note, however, that in this business earnings can vary greatly from month to month, depending on how many fugitives the bounty hunter is able to bring in, the bail bond for these fugitives, and expenses incurred in the process. Well-established bail enforcement agents with excellent reputations often get the highest-paying cases, such as for a fugitive who has run on a $100,000 bail, and may find their yearly earnings approaching the $100,000 mark.

Because they own their own businesses, most bail enforcement agents do not receive medical benefits. A few who work for well-established agencies may receive some types of benefits, but it is not the norm for the field. "In this business, sometimes it is slow or there is no business, and there are lengthy times between paychecks. There are also no benefits like pensions, insurance, or things of that nature in most cases," says John Norman.

WORK ENVIRONMENT

Bounty hunters spend much of their time traveling in search of a fugitive or waiting for hours for a fugitive to appear. Because apprehending a fugitive is easiest in the middle of the night or early morning, the bounty hunter keeps odd hours and may work especially long hours when close to capturing a fugitive. A bail enforcement agent works on an as-needed basis, so there may be stretches of inactivity depending on the bondsman's needs for service. The number of hours worked varies with the number of fugitives being sought at any one time and the amount of time remaining to bring the fugitive in. Bounty hunters are often in perilous situations where injury or even death is a possibility. John Norman describes bail enforcement as a "painstaking, unforgiving business."

OUTLOOK

Employment for bounty hunters is increasing about as fast as the average for all other occupations, although this field has a narrow niche in the bail bonding business. Competition among bail enforcement agents continues to propel the field as a profession and as an asset to our legal system. Because bail bond agents and bail enforcement agents are working in private business, there is no cost to the taxpayer for the apprehension of these fugitives (as there would be if, for example, police officers worked exclusively on these cases). Another benefit of the private bail enforcement agent system is its high success rate (some professionals estimate it at 85 percent) for recovery of fugitives. Given the large percentage of recoveries and the lack of cost to local government, the future looks good for this profession. The ability of bail enforcement agents to work successfully within the parameters of the law should keep this field growing steadily in the future.

FOR MORE INFORMATION

Visit the Bail Bond Recovery Resource Center of The National Association of Investigative Specialists, Inc., Web site. The resource center has information on the work of bounty hunters, laws affecting bounty hunting, and training materials.

Bail Bond Recovery Resource Center
The National Association of Investigative Specialists, Inc.
PO Box 82148
Austin, TX 78708-2148
Tel: 512-719-3595
http://www.pimall.com/nais/bailr.html

For training information and to read sections from the newsletter Hunters Net, *visit the NABEA Web site.*

National Association of Bail Enforcement Agents (NABEA)
PO Box 129
Falls Church, VA 22040-0129
Tel: 703-534-4211
http://www.nabea.org

For information about fugitive recovery seminars, contact
National Institute of Bail Enforcement
PO Box 667
Spring Grove, IL 60081-0667
Tel: 815-675-0260
http://www.bounty-hunter.net

Corrections Officers

OVERVIEW

Corrections officers guard people who have been arrested and are awaiting trial or who have been tried, convicted, and sentenced to serve time in a penal institution. They search prisoners and their cells for weapons, drugs, and other contraband; inspect windows, doors, locks, and gates for signs of tampering; observe the conduct and behavior of inmates to prevent disturbances or escapes; and make verbal or written reports to superior officers. Corrections officers assign work to inmates and supervise their activities. They guard prisoners who are being transported between jails, courthouses, mental institutions, or other destinations, and supervise prisoners receiving visitors. When necessary, these workers use weapons or force to maintain discipline and order. There are approximately 484,000 corrections officers employed in the United States.

HISTORY

For centuries, punishment for criminal behavior was generally left in the hands of the injured individual or his or her relatives. This resulted in blood feuds, which could carry on for years and which eventually could be resolved by the payment of money to the victim or the victim's family. When kingdoms emerged as the standard form of government, certain actions came to be regarded as an affront to the king or the peace of his domain, and the king assumed the responsibility for punishing the wrongs committed by a subject or his clan. In this way, crime became a public offense. The earliest corrections officers were more likely to be executioners and torturers than guards or jailers.

QUICK FACTS

School Subjects
Government
Physical education
Psychology

Personal Skills
Communication/ideas
Helping/teaching

Work Environment
Primarily indoors
Primarily one location

Minimum Education Level
High school diploma

Salary Range
$23,010 to $34,090 to $55,530+

Certification or Licensing
Required by certain states

Outlook
More slowly than the average

DOT
372

GOE
04.03.01

NOC
6462

O*NET-SOC
33-1011.00, 33-3012.00

Early criminals were treated inhumanely. They were often put to death for minor offenses, exiled, forced into hard labor, given corporal punishment, tortured, mutilated, turned into slaves, or left to rot in dungeons. Jailing criminals was not considered a penalty in and of itself, but rather as a temporary measure until punishment could be carried out. More often, prisons were established to punish debtors or to house orphans and delinquent youths. One of the earliest debtor's prisons was Bridewell, in London, England, which was established in 1553. Other European countries built similar institutions.

During the Enlightenment of the 18th century, the belief that punishment alone deters crime began to weaken. The practice of imprisonment became more and more common as attempts were made to fit the degree of punishment to the nature of the crime. Societies looked to deter crime with the promise of clear and just punishment. Rehabilitation of offenders was to be achieved through isolation, hard labor, penitence, and discipline. By 1829, prisoners in most prisons were required to perform hard labor, which proved more cost-effective for the prison systems. Before long, the rehabilitation aspect of imprisonment became less important than the goal of simply isolating prisoners from society and creating respect for authority and order. Prisoners were subjected to harsh treatment from generally untrained personnel.

By 1870, calls for prison reform introduced new sentencing procedures such as parole and probation. It was hoped that providing opportunities for early release would provide prisoners with more incentive toward rehabilitation. Prisons evolved into several types, providing minimum, medium, and maximum security. The role of the prison guard at each institution evolved accordingly. The recognition of prisoners' rights also provided new limitations and purposes for the conduct and duties of the prison guard. Corrections officers began to receive specialized training in the treatment and rehabilitation of prisoners.

Until the 1980s, corrections officers were employees of the federal, state, or local government. A dramatic increase in the number of prisoners, brought on by the so-called War on Drugs, led to overcrowded prisons and skyrocketing costs. At the same time, the system itself came under attack, especially the concepts of parole and reduced sentencing. Many states began to contract private companies to build and operate additional correctional facilities. Today, corrections officers are employed at every level of government and often by these private companies.

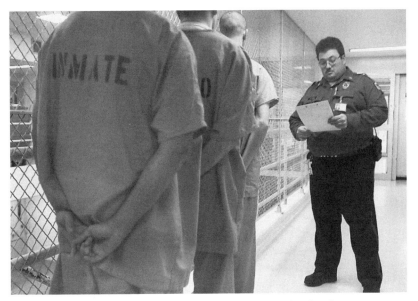

Oklahoma corrections officer Sgt. John Thomas checks the inmates he is moving to another area of the prison's assessment center. *(J. Pat Carter/AP)*

THE JOB

To prevent disturbances or escapes, corrections officers carefully observe the conduct and behavior of the inmates at all times. They watch for forbidden activities and infractions of the rules, as well as for poor attitudes or unsatisfactory adjustment to prison life on the part of the inmates. They try to settle disputes before violence can erupt. They may search the prisoners or their living quarters for weapons or drugs and inspect locks, bars on windows and doors, and gates for any evidence of tampering. The inmates are under guard constantly while eating, sleeping, exercising, bathing, and working. They are counted periodically to be sure all are present. Some officers are stationed on towers and at gates to prevent escapes. All rule-violations and anything out of the ordinary are reported to a superior officer such as a chief jailer. In case of a major disturbance, corrections officers may use weapons or force to restore order.

Corrections officers give work assignments to prisoners, supervise them as they carry out their duties, and instruct them in unfamiliar tasks. Corrections officers are responsible for the physical needs of the prisoners, such as providing or obtaining meals and medical aid.

They assure the health and safety of the inmates by checking the cells for unsanitary conditions and fire hazards.

These workers may escort inmates from their cells to the prison's visiting room, medical office, or chapel. Certain officers, called *patrol conductors*, guard prisoners who are being transported between courthouses, prisons, mental institutions, or other destinations, either by van, car, or public transportation. Officers at a penal institution may also screen visitors at the entrance and accompany them to other areas within the facility. From time to time, they may inspect mail addressed to prisoners, checking for contraband; help investigate crimes committed within the prison; or aid in the search for escapees.

Some police officers specialize in guarding juvenile offenders being held at a police station house or detention room pending a hearing, transfer to a correctional institution, or return to their parents. They often investigate the backgrounds of first offenders to check for a criminal history or to make a recommendation to the magistrate regarding disposition of the case. Lost or runaway children are also placed in the care of these officers until their parents or guardians can be located.

Immigration guards guard aliens held by the immigration service awaiting investigation, deportation, or release. *Gate tenders* check the identification of all persons entering and leaving the penal institution.

In most correctional institutions, *psychologists* and *social workers* are employed to counsel inmates with mental and emotional problems. It is an important part of a corrections officer's job, however, to supplement this with informal counseling. Officers may help inmates adjust to prison life, prepare for return to civilian life, and avoid committing crimes in the future. On a more immediate level, they may arrange for an inmate to visit the library, help inmates get in touch with their families, suggest where to look for a job after release from prison, or discuss personal problems. In some institutions, corrections officers may lead more formal group counseling sessions. As they fulfill more rehabilitative roles, corrections officers are increasingly required to possess a college-level education in psychology, criminology, or related areas of study.

Corrections officers keep a daily record of their activities and make regular reports, either verbal or written, to their supervisors. These reports concern the behavior of the inmates and the quality and quantity of work they do, as well as any disturbances, rule violations, and unusual occurrences that may have taken place.

Head corrections officers supervise and coordinate other corrections officers. They perform roll call and assign duties to the officers; direct the activities of groups of inmates; arrange the release and transfer of prisoners in accordance with the instructions on a court order; maintain security and investigate disturbances among the inmates; maintain prison records and prepare reports; and review and evaluate the performance of their subordinates.

In small communities, corrections officers (who are sometimes called *jailers*) may also act as deputy sheriffs or police officers when they are not occupied with guard duties.

REQUIREMENTS

High School
To work as a corrections officer, candidates generally must meet the minimum age requirement—usually 18 or 21—and have a high school diploma or its equivalent. Individuals without a high school education may be considered for employment if they have qualifying work experience, such as probation and parole experience.

Postsecondary Training
Many states and correctional facilities prefer or require officers to have postsecondary training in psychology, criminology, or related areas of study. Some states require applicants to have one or two years of previous experience in corrections or related police work. Some state governments also require military or related work experience. On the federal level, applicants should have at least two years of college or two years of work or military experience.

Training for corrections officers ranges from the special academy instruction provided by the federal government and some states to the informal, on-the-job training furnished by most states and local governments. The Federal Bureau of Prisons operates a training center in Glynco, Georgia, where new hires generally undergo a three-week program of basic corrections education. Training academies have programs that last from four to eight weeks and instruct trainees on institutional policies, regulations, and procedures; the behavior and custody of inmates; security measures; and report writing. Training in self-defense, the use of firearms and other weapons, and emergency medical techniques is often provided. On-the-job trainees spend two to six months or more under the supervision of an experienced officer. During that period of time, they receive in-house training while gaining actual experience. Periodically, corrections officers may be given additional training as new ideas and procedures in criminal justice are developed.

Certification or Licensing

Numerous certification programs are available to corrections officers; these are optional in most states. Common certifications include self-defense, weapons use, urine analysis, shield and gun, shotgun/handgun, CPR, and cell extraction. Many officers also take advantage of additional training that is offered at their facility, such as suicide prevention, AIDS awareness, use of four-point restraints, and emergency preparedness. At most prisons, there is annual mandatory in-service training that focuses on policies and procedures. The American Correctional Association and the American Jail Association offer certification programs to corrections officers and corrections managers.

Corrections officers who work for the federal government and most state governments are covered by civil service systems or merit boards and may be required to pass a competitive exam for employment. Many states require random or comprehensive drug testing of their officers, either during hiring procedures or while employed at the facility.

Other Requirements

There is no denying that handling the inherent stress of this line of work takes a unique person. In a maximum-security facility, the environment is often noisy, crowded, poorly ventilated, and even dangerous. Corrections officers need the physical and emotional strength to handle the stress involved in working with criminals, some of whom may be violent. A corrections officer has to stay alert and aware of prisoners' actions and attitudes. This constant vigilance can be harder on some people. Work in a minimum-security prison is usually more comfortable, cleaner, and less stressful.

Officers need to use persuasion rather than brute force to get inmates to follow the rules. Certain inmates take a disproportionate amount of time and attention because they are either violent, mentally ill, or victims of abuse by other inmates. Officers have to carry out routine duties while being alert for the unpredictable outbursts. Sound judgment and the ability to think and act quickly are important qualities for corrections officers. With experience and training, corrections officers are usually able to handle volatile situations without resorting to physical force.

The ability to communicate clearly verbally and in writing is extremely important. Corrections officers have to write a number of reports, documenting routine procedures as well as any violations by the inmates. A correction officer's eight-hour shift can easily extend to 10 hours because of the reports that must be written.

An effective corrections officer is not easily intimidated or influenced by the inmates. There is a misconception, however, that corrections officers need to be tough guys. While it's true that a person needs some physical strength to perform the job, corrections officers also need to be able to use their head to anticipate and defuse any potentially dangerous situations between inmates or between guards and inmates.

Most correctional institutions require candidates to be at least 18 years old (sometimes 21 years old), have a high school diploma, and be a U.S. citizen with no criminal record. There are also health and physical strength requirements, and many states have minimum height, vision, and hearing standards. Other common requirements are a driver's license and a job record that shows you've been dependable.

EXPLORING

Because of age requirements and the nature of the work, there are no opportunities for high school students to gain actual experience while still in school. Where the minimum age requirement is 21, prospective corrections officers may prepare for employment by taking college courses in criminal justice or police science. Enrollment in a two- or four-year college degree program in a related field is encouraged. Military service may also offer experience and training in corrections. Social work is another way to gain experience. You may also look into obtaining a civilian job as a clerk or other worker for the police department or other protective service organization. Related part-time, volunteer, or summer work may also be available in psychiatric hospitals and other institutions that provide physical and emotional counseling and services. Many online services also have forums for corrections officers and other public safety employees, and these may provide opportunities to read about and communicate with people active in this career.

EMPLOYERS

Most corrections officers work for the government at the local, state, and federal levels in penal institutions and in jobs connected with the penal system. Of the approximately 484,000 corrections officers employed in the United States, roughly 60 percent work in state-run correctional facilities such as prisons, prison camps, and

Lingo to Learn

Contraband: Any forbidden item that is in a prisoner's possession.

House: An inmate will refer to his cell as his "house."

Run: A hallway lined with inmates' cells.

Shake-down: Corrections officers conduct a thorough search of an inmate's cell, looking for contraband.

Yard-out: This means that it's time for the inmates to go to the yard for exercise. Correctional officers also say "chow-out" when it's time for the inmates to eat and "shower-out" when it's time for showers.

reformatories. Most of the rest are employed at city and county jails or other institutions. Roughly 16,000 work for the federal government and approximately 15,000 work for private corrections contractors.

STARTING OUT

To apply for a job as a corrections officer, contact federal or state civil service commissions, state departments of correction, or local correctional facilities and ask for information about entrance requirements, training, and job opportunities. Private contractors and other companies are also a growing source of employment opportunities. Many officers enter this field from social work areas and parole and probation positions.

ADVANCEMENT

Many officers take college courses in law enforcement or criminal justice to increase their chances of promotion. In some states, officers must serve two years in each position before they can be considered for a promotion.

With additional education and training, experienced officers can also be promoted to supervisory or administrative positions such as head corrections officer, assistant warden, or prison director. Officers who want to continue to work directly with offenders can move into various other positions. For example, *probation and parole officers* monitor and counsel offenders, process their release from prison, and evaluate their progress in becoming productive members of society. *Recreation leaders* organize and instruct offenders in sports, games, and arts and crafts.

EARNINGS

Wages for corrections officers vary considerably depending on their employers and their level of experience. According to the U.S. Department of Labor, the 2005 median annual earnings for corrections officers employed by the federal government were $45,960; for those employed by state governments, $37,220; and for those employed by local governments, $35,620. The U.S. Department of Labor reports that overall the lowest paid 10 percent of corrections officers earned less than $23,010 per year in 2005, and the highest paid 10 percent earned more than $55,530. Median earnings for corrections officers were $34,090.

The U.S. Department of Labor reports higher earnings for first-line supervisors/managers, with a median yearly income of $48,570 in 2005. The lowest paid 10 percent earned less than $30,640, and the highest paid 10 percent earned more than $75,350.

Overtime, night shift, weekend, and holiday pay differentials are generally available at most institutions. Fringe benefits may include health, disability, and life insurance; uniforms or a cash allowance to buy their own uniforms; and sometimes meals and housing. Officers who work for the federal government and for most state governments are covered by civil service systems or merit boards. Some corrections officers also receive retirement and pension plans, and retirement is often possible after 20 to 25 years of service.

WORK ENVIRONMENT

Because prison security must be maintained around the clock, work schedules for corrections officers may include nights, weekends, and holidays. The workweek, however, generally consists of five days, eight hours per day, except during emergencies, when many officers work overtime.

Corrections officers may work indoors or outdoors, depending on their duties. Conditions can vary even within an institution: Some areas are well lighted, ventilated, and temperature-controlled, while others are overcrowded, hot, and noisy. Officers who work outdoors, of course, are subject to all kinds of weather. Correctional institutions occasionally present unpredictable or even hazardous situations. If violence erupts among the inmates, corrections officers may be in danger of injury or death. Although this risk is higher than for most other occupations, corrections work is usually routine.

Corrections officers need physical and emotional strength to cope with the stress inherent in dealing with criminals, many of whom may be dangerous or incapable of change. A correctional officer has to remain alert and aware of the surroundings, prisoners' movements and attitudes, and any potential for danger or violence. Such continual, heightened levels of alertness often create psychological stress for some workers. Most institutions have stress-reduction programs or seminars for their employees, but if not, insurance usually covers some form of therapy for work-related stress.

OUTLOOK

Employment in this field is expected to grow more slowly than the average for all occupations through 2014, according to the U.S. Department of Labor. Despite this prediction, there should be thousands of job openings annually for qualified workers. The ongoing prosecution of illegal drugs, new tough-on-crime legislation, and increasing mandatory sentencing policies will create a need for more prison beds and more corrections officers. The extremely crowded conditions in today's correctional institutions have created a need for more corrections officers to guard the inmates more closely and relieve the tensions. A greater number of officers will also be required as a result of the expansion or new construction of facilities. As prison sentences become longer through mandatory minimum sentences set by state law, the number of prisons needed will increase. In addition, many job openings will occur from a characteristically high turnover rate, as well as from the need to fill vacancies caused by the death or retirement of older workers. Traditionally, corrections agencies have difficulty attracting qualified employees due to job location and salary considerations.

Because security must be maintained at correctional facilities at all times, corrections officers can depend on steady employment. They are not usually affected by poor economic conditions or changes in government spending. Corrections officers are rarely laid off, even when budgets need to be trimmed. Instead, because of high turnovers, staffs can be cut simply by not replacing those officers who leave.

Most jobs will be found in relatively large institutions located near metropolitan areas, although opportunities for corrections officers exist in jails and other smaller facilities throughout the country. The increasing use of private companies and privately run prisons may limit somewhat the growth of jobs in this field as these companies are more likely to keep a close eye on the bottom line. Use of new technologies, such as surveillance equipment, automatic gates, and other devices, may also allow institutions to employ fewer officers.

FOR MORE INFORMATION

For information on training, conferences, and membership, contact

American Correctional Association
206 North Washington Street, Suite 200
Alexandria, VA 22314-2528
Tel: 703-224-0000
http://www.aca.org

American Probation and Parole Association
2760 Research Park Drive
Lexington, KY 40511-8410
Tel: 859-244-8203
Email: appa@csg.org
http://www.appa-net.org

For information on entrance requirements, training, and career opportunities for corrections officers at the federal level, contact

Federal Bureau of Prisons
320 First Street, NW
Washington, DC 20534-0002
Tel: 202-307-3198
http://www.bop.gov

This Web site bills itself as the "Largest Online Resource for News and Information in Corrections."

The Corrections Connection
http://www.corrections.com

Crime Analysts

QUICK FACTS

School Subjects
Computer science
English
Psychology

Personal Skills
Helping/teaching
Technical/scientific

Work Environment
Primarily indoors
Primarily multiple locations

Minimum Education Level
Bachelor's degree

Salary Range
$15,500 to $35,650 to
$71,593+

Certification or Licensing
Voluntary

Outlook
Faster than the average

DOT
029

GOE
04.03.02

NOC
N/A

O*NET-SOC
19-4092.00

OVERVIEW

Crime analysts analyze patterns in criminal behavior in order to catch criminals, predict patterns and motives of criminals, and improve the responsiveness of law enforcement agencies.

HISTORY

Crime has always been a major social problem, especially in heavily populated areas. Police and other law enforcement officials work to detect and apprehend criminals and protect citizens from robbery, violence, and other criminal acts. They are assisted by crime analysts— civilian workers who are hired to study crime statistics and patterns in order to give law enforcement officials an extra edge in fighting crime.

The earliest crime analysts simply analyzed raw crime statistics. Today, crime analysts use computer software, databases, and geographic information systems to predict and even prevent crimes. In recent years, crime analysis has become a popular career choice. This new technology and the emergence of community-oriented policing —which puts officers on the streets as opposed to behind a desk—have created many new opportunities for trained crime analysts.

THE JOB

Crime analysts try to uncover and piece together information about crime patterns, crime trends, and criminal suspects. It is a job that varies widely from day to day and from one state and law enforcement agency to the next. At its core is a systematic process that involves collecting, categorizing, analyzing, and sharing information in order to help the agency that a crime analyst works for to better deploy officers on the street, work through difficult investigations, and increase arrests of criminals.

The basic work of a crime analyst involves collecting crime data from a range of sources, including police reports, statewide computer databases, crime newsletters, word-of-mouth tips, and interviews with suspects. To be useful, this information is then analyzed for patterns. Crime analysts are constantly vigilant for details that are similar or familiar. In addition to specific crime data, a crime analyst might study general factors such as population density, the demographic makeup of the population, commuting patterns, economic conditions (average income, poverty level, job availability), effectiveness of law enforcement agencies, citizens' attitudes toward crime, and crime reporting practices.

"You get a feel for it after a while," says Michelle Rankin, who heads a police department's crime analysis unit in Santa Clara, a town of more than 100,000 in northern California. She tells of reading a teletype recently that described a suspect in a bank robbery. "Something about the description of his nose and hairline rang a bell," she says. By combing through some old teletypes, she found a similar description and called the agency that had arrested the man before. In doing so, she was able to uncover the man's name and obtain a photo of him that matched a surveillance photo from the bank.

The responsibilities of crime analysts are often dependent upon the needs of their police department or law enforcement agency. One morning's tasks might include writing a profile on a particular demographic group's criminal patterns. On another day, an analyst could meet with the police chief to discuss an unusual string of local car thefts. Less frequently, the work includes going on "ride-alongs" with street cops, visiting a crime scene, or meeting with crime analysts from surrounding jurisdictions to exchange information about criminals who are plaguing the region. Occasionally, a crime analyst is pulled off of everyday responsibilities in order to work exclusively on a task force, usually focusing on a rash of violent crimes. As an ongoing responsibility, a crime analyst might be charged with tracking and monitoring "known offenders" (sex offenders, career criminals, repeat juvenile offenders, and parolees).

New computer technology has had a profound impact on the profession of crime analysis, helping it grow by leaps and bounds. In its earliest days, crime analysis simply meant gathering straight statistics on crime. Now, these same statistics—coupled with specialized software—allow crime analysts to actually anticipate and prevent criminal activity.

The use of this analysis falls into three broad categories: *tactical, strategic,* and *administrative.* Tactical crime analysis aims at giving police officers and detectives prompt, in-the-field information that could lead to an arrest. These are the "hot" items that land on a crime analyst's desk, usually pertaining to specific crimes and offenders. For example, a criminal's mode of operation (M.O.) can be studied in order to predict who the likely next targets or victims will be. The police can then set up stakeouts or saturate the area with patrol cars. Tactical analysis is also used to do crime-suspect correlation, which involves identifying suspects for certain crimes based on their criminal histories.

Strategic analysis deals with finding solutions to long-range problems and crime trends. For instance, a crime analyst could create a crime trend forecast, based on current and past criminal activity, using computer software. An analyst might also perform a "manpower deployment" study to see if the police department is making the best use of its personnel. Another aspect of strategic analysis involves collating and disseminating demographic data on victims and geographic areas experiencing high crime rates so that the police are able to beef up crime prevention efforts.

Lastly, administrative analysis helps to provide policy-making information to a police department's administration. This might include a statistical study on the activity levels of police officers that would support a request for hiring more officers. Administrative work could also include creating graphs and charts that are used in management presentations or writing a speech on local crime prevention to give to the city council.

REQUIREMENTS

High School

While there are still a few law enforcement agencies that will hire crime analysts with only a high school diploma, it is becoming less common. Judy Kimminau, who works for the police department in Fort Collins, Colorado, says, "Crime analysis used to be a field that a person could stray into, but most new analysts now are trained or educated specifically for the career."

Michelle Rankin adds: "While you're finishing up high school, it pays to hone your writing skills. You have to understand different styles of communicating so that you're able to write to the street cop and also to the city council." A good foundation in algebra will help with statistics classes in college. Moreover, take advantage of your school's computer lab, as basic knowledge of computers, word processing, spreadsheets, and databases is important.

Postsecondary Training

The majority of agencies require a bachelor's degree for the position of crime analyst. Rankin earned her bachelor's degree in criminal justice, but it was not until her senior year of college that she actually learned about the field of crime analysis. "I had been trying to figure out how I wanted to use my degree. Then a senior seminar course in crime analysis was offered—the first of its kind. It sparked my interest and I began volunteering in my instructor's unit." When a job opened in the unit, Rankin applied and was hired. Kimminau, on the other hand, learned about crime analysis in high school and designed a personalized degree in criminology accordingly. Other excellent degrees to consider include statistics, criminal justice, computer science, and sociology.

Both Rankin and Kimminau agree that an internship during college is the best way to get a foot in the door and gain on-the-job experience. "Because of lean staffing, most units rely heavily on interns for support. The best thing is to contact a unit and talk with the crime analyst there," says Kimminau. She adds that a strong candidate for an internship would be organized, computer-literate, and have a basic understanding of statistics. In her unit, interns initially begin by reading police reports, learning how to glean significant facts and patterns from them. "It's pretty exciting the first time a spark goes off and an intern says, 'Hey, there's a pattern here!'"

Certification or Licensing

Currently, only California and Florida offer a formal, state-sponsored certification program for crime analysts. Individuals take 40 hours of courses on subjects such as crime analysis, criminal intelligence analysis, investigative analysis, and law enforcement research methods and statistics.

The Society of Certified Criminal Analysts also offers two levels of certification: regular and lifetime. Candidates for regular certification must have two years of college education, be a working analyst, and successfully complete a written and practical test. Those who have earned the regular certification must recertify every three years. Candidates for lifetime certification must have four years of college and 10 years of "analytical experience" in the field. The

International Association of Crime Analysts offers the certified law enforcement analyst designation to applicants with three years of experience who pass an examination.

Other Requirements

Crime analysts need to be inquisitive, logical, and have a good memory for what they hear and read. A willingness to dig in and do this sort of research is also important, since much of the work involves piecing together disparate bits of information. Ask Steven Gottlieb, MPA, an internationally recognized crime analysis trainer, consultant, and executive director of the Alpha Group Center for Crime and Intelligence Analysis, just who will make a good crime analyst and he laughs, "Somebody who does crossword puzzles in ink." He explains that crime analysts love the process of working with bits of data that in and of themselves mean nothing. "It's only when you put them together that a clear picture emerges," he says.

Even though crime analysts are not out on the streets, they are immersed in the law enforcement milieu and come into contact with information that's potentially disturbing. "If a person becomes especially upset after reading in the newspaper reports on a murder or a child's molestation, or after seeing a crime scene photo on television," notes Judy Kimminau, "they're probably not cut out for this line of work."

It is important to note that a crime analyst has to be willing to work in the background and not always be in the limelight. The positive side is that a crime analyst plays a significant role in all of the big cases, but does not have to wear a bulletproof vest in 100-degree heat or direct traffic in the rain. "You can play cop without the danger," jokes Michelle Rankin.

EXPLORING

There are plenty of ways that you can begin your own training and education now. First of all, get some exposure to the law enforcement community by volunteering at the local police department. Many towns have a Boy Scouts Explorers program in which students (of both sexes) work to educate themselves about law enforcement.

EMPLOYERS

The majority of crime analysts are employed by local and state law enforcement agencies. A great number are also hired by federal agencies such as the Federal Bureau of Investigation (FBI), the Bureau of Customs and Border Protection, and the Department of Justice. In addition, some private security firms hire people with training in crime analysis.

STARTING OUT

While there is not a single, central clearinghouse for all crime analyst jobs, there are several places to look for listings. By becoming a member of the International Association of Crime Analysts (IACA), you will receive a newsletter that includes job openings. Judy Kimminau also advises finding out if there is a state association of crime analysts where you live and attend meetings, if possible. However, recent graduates would be best advised to be willing to move out of state if the job pickings are slim locally.

The key to getting a job in the field is doing an internship in college (see "Postsecondary Training"). In the past six months, Kimminau has assisted several agencies that are hiring crime analysts for the first time. "It's not unusual for recent college graduates to be hired, but all of these people had done internships." Michelle Rankin adds that a new crime analyst would have a solid shot at finding a

Crime Confusion

In a field like crime analysis, there's sometimes confusion about who does what. The quickest way to tick off a crime analyst is to say something about their lab coats. (Hint: They don't wear lab coats, nor do they spend their days in laboratories.) So, here are a few professions with titles that might sound a lot like crime analyst, but are actually different careers:

- *Crime scene evidence technicians* go to the scene of the crime in order to collect and photograph relevant evidence, such as fingerprints, hairs, bullets, etc.
- *Criminalists* scientifically analyze, compare, and evaluate physical evidence in the laboratory.
- *Criminologists* study and research crime from a sociological perspective. They usually work in a university setting, rather than for a law enforcement agency.
- *Forensic psychologists* make psychological evaluations based on criminal evidence or behavior.

job in a larger, established unit where he or she could volunteer first, learning from someone with greater experience.

ADVANCEMENT

As a broad generalization, most crime analysts are not pushing and shoving to climb the career ladder. Since theirs is often a one- or two-person, nonhierarchical unit within an agency, they more likely chose crime analysis because they relish the nature of the work itself. Obviously, advancement possibilities depend largely on the size and structure of the agency for which a crime analyst works. In larger agencies, there are sometimes senior analysts, supervising analysts, or crime analysis managers. Some of these positions require a master's degree.

More often, crime analysts set their sights on increasing the impact they have on the agency and community in which they work. Michelle Rankin says she sees herself staying in Santa Clara's unit and helping to establish a regional approach to crime analysis. "In the Bay Area, each agency has its own crime analysis unit and its own information system," she explains. "I'd like to work toward combining these resources and linking the individual systems."

Two careers that are closely linked to crime analysts are *criminal intelligence analyst* and *investigative analyst*. Criminal intelligence analysis involves the study of relationships between people, organizations, and events; it focuses on organized crime, money laundering, and other conspiratorial crimes. Investigative analysis attempts to uncover why a person is committing serial crimes such as murder and rape. Getting into the field of investigative analysis (sometimes called *profiling*) usually requires years of experience and additional education in psychology—as well as good instincts.

EARNINGS

Earnings for crime analysts vary considerably, based on factors such as the location, the size of the employing agency and its financial status, and the analyst's experience. The IACA reports that salaries ranged from a low of $15,500 to a high of $71,593 in 2002. The mean salary reported was $35,650. Crime/Intelligence analyst supervisors averaged $44,680.

Analysts receive the same benefits as others working in the same agency. These usually include paid vacation time, sick leave, health insurance, and retirement plans.

WORK ENVIRONMENT

The duties of crime analysts will vary based on the requirements of the law enforcement agency for which they work. Analysts ordinarily work in the office analyzing crime information; occasionally, though, they may go on a "ride-along" with police officers or visit a crime scene to gather more information. Crime scenes can often be disturbing, and crime analysts need to act in a professional manner in these situations.

Analysts are constantly in communication with police chiefs, officers in the field, and fellow crime analysts as they work on a case. They need to establish good working relationships with officers who sometimes initially resent working with a civilian employee. "Sometimes I'll come up with a good lead, but the officer on the beat doesn't take it up," Michelle Rankin says. "You need to have tough skin and focus on working with those who want to work with you."

OUTLOOK

As the job of the crime analyst becomes increasingly well-known and as analysts' work continues to contribute to positive results for law enforcement agencies, the need for these professionals should grow. One factor that has added to the need for crime analysts is the emergence of community-oriented policing. The point of this type of policing is to get police officers out on the streets of their communities rather than doing paperwork at a desk. To do this, many agencies are hiring civilians for desk jobs, which allows more police officers to be a presence in their community. Michelle Rankin comments, "You want to put somebody behind a desk who actually wants to be there. The push in many departments is to 'civilianize' job functions so that police officers can work smarter, not harder." Crime analysis makes good use of the information that police officers collect on the streets. "With a limited number of officers, departments have to ask, 'What's the best use of their time?'" says Steven Gottlieb. "Good crime analysis helps to deploy officers in the right places at the right times."

The field is also growing because better software is becoming available. "Statistics are age-old," Gottlieb says, "but doing them by hand was cumbersome. The newest technology—like sophisticated databases and geographic mapping systems—gives us increased capabilities."

While this growth trend is expected to continue, it is important to recognize that it is still a competitive job market. Those who want to become crime analysts should be willing to move to find an agency with a job opening. They should also bear in mind that police departments are historically more likely to lay off a civilian than a street officer.

FOR MORE INFORMATION

For information on careers in criminology, contact
American Society of Criminology
1314 Kinnear Road, Suite 212
Columbus, OH 43212-1156
Tel: 614-292-9207
http://www.asc41.com

For information on membership, contact
International Association of Crime Analysts
9218 Metcalf Avenue, #364
Overland Park, KS 66212-1476
Tel: 800-609-3419
http://www.iaca.net

For information on certification, contact
Society of Certified Criminal Analysts
c/o Ed Feingold, CCA
Bureau of Alcohol, Tobacco, Firearms and Explosives
Phoenix Division, Intel Group IV
201 East Washington Street, Suite 940
Phoenix, AZ 85004-2467
http://www.certifiedanalysts.net

Customs Officials

OVERVIEW

Customs officials are federal workers who are employed by the United States Bureau of Customs and Border Protection (an arm of the Department of Homeland Security) to prevent terrorists and terrorist weapons from entering the United States, enforce laws governing imports and exports, and to combat smuggling and revenue fraud. The Bureau of Customs and Border Protection generates revenue for the government by assessing and collecting duties and excise taxes on imported merchandise. Amid a whirl of international travel and commercial activity, customs officials process travelers, baggage, cargo, and mail, as well as administer certain navigation laws. Stationed in the United States and overseas at airports, seaports, and all crossings, as well as at points along the Canadian and Mexican borders, customs officials examine, count, weigh, gauge, measure, and sample commercial and noncommercial cargoes entering and leaving the United States. It is their job to determine whether or not goods are admissible and, if so, how much tax, or duty, should be assessed on them. To prevent smuggling, fraud, and cargo theft, customs officials also check the individual baggage declarations of international travelers and oversee the unloading of all types of commercial shipments. More than 40,000 customs workers are employed by the Bureau of Customs and Border Protection.

QUICK FACTS

School Subjects
English
Government

Personal Skills
Communication/ideas
Helping/teaching

Work Environment
Primarily indoors
Primarily one location

Minimum Education Level
High school diploma

Salary Range
$25,195 to $46,189 to $55,360+

Certification or Licensing
None available

Outlook
About as fast as the average

DOT
168

GOE
04.03.01

NOC
1236

O*NET-SOC
33-3021.05

HISTORY

Countries collect taxes on imports and sometimes on exports as a means of producing revenue for the government. Export duties were first introduced in England in the year 1275 by a statute that levied taxes on animal hides and on wool. American colonists in the 1700s objected to the import duties England forced them to pay (levied under the Townshend Acts), charging "taxation without representation." Although the British government rescinded the Townshend Acts, it retained the tax on tea, which led to the Boston Tea Party on December 16, 1773.

After the American Revolution, delegates at the Constitutional Convention decided that "no tax or duty shall be laid on articles exported from any state," but they approved taxing imports from abroad. The First Congress in 1789 established the customs service as part of the Treasury Department. Until 1816, these customs assessments were used primarily for revenue. The Tariff Act of 1816 declared, however, that the main function of customs laws was to protect American industry from foreign companies. By 1927 the customs service was established as a separate bureau within the Treasury Department.

Customs and Border Protection officer Mary Armbrust uses the new US-VISIT biometric program on a visitor from Brazil. The system fingerprints and photographs visitors to the United States who require visas. *(Getty Images)*

The terrorist attacks of 2001 prompted a restructuring of many governmental agencies, including the U.S. Customs Service. In 2003, the U.S. Customs Service was renamed the Bureau of Customs and Border Protection (CBP) and merged with portions of the Department of Agriculture, the Immigration and Naturalization Service, and the Border Patrol. CBP became an official agency of the Department of Homeland Security on March 1, 2003.

Today, the Bureau of Customs and Border Protection oversees more than 400 laws and regulations and generates more government money than any other federal agency besides the Internal Revenue Service.

THE JOB

Customs officials perform a wide variety of duties including preventing terrorists and terrorist weapons from entering the United States, controlling imports and exports, and combating smuggling and revenue fraud.

As a result of its merger in 2003 with several other protective and monitoring agencies of the U.S. government, the Bureau of Customs and Border Patrol has created a new position, the *Customs and Border Patrol (CBP) Officer,* which consolidates the skills and responsibilities of three positions in these agencies: the customs inspector, the immigration officer, and the agricultural inspector. These workers are uniformed and armed. A second new position, the *CBP Agriculture Specialist,* has been created to complement the work of the CBP Officer. CBP Agriculture Specialists are uniformed, but not armed.

CBP Officers conduct surveillance at points of entry into the United States to prohibit smuggling, detect customs violations, and deter acts of terrorism. They try to catch people illegally transporting smuggled merchandise and contraband such as narcotics, watches, jewelry, chemicals, and weapons, as well as fruits, plants, and meat that may be infested with pests or diseases. On the waterfront, officers monitor piers, ships, and crew members and are constantly on the lookout for items being thrown from the ship to small boats nearby. Customs patrol officers provide security at entrance and exit facilities of piers and airports, make sure all baggage is checked, and maintain security at loading, exit, and entrance areas of customs buildings and during the transfer of legal drug shipments to prevent hijackings or theft. Using informers and other sources, they gather intelligence information about illegal activities. When probable cause exists, they are authorized to take possible violators into custody, using physical force or weapons if necessary. They assist other customs personnel in developing or testing new enforcement techniques and equipment.

CBP Officers are also responsible for carefully and thoroughly examining cargo to make sure that it matches the description on a ship's or aircraft's manifest. They inspect baggage and personal items worn or carried by travelers entering or leaving the United States by ship, plane, or automobile. CBP Officers are authorized to go aboard a ship or plane to determine the exact nature of the cargo being transported. In the course of a single day they review cargo manifests, inspect cargo containers, and supervise unloading activities to prevent terrorism, smuggling, fraud, or cargo thefts. They may have to weigh and measure imports to see that commerce laws are being followed and to protect American distributors in cases where restricted, trademarked merchandise is being brought into the country. In this way, they can protect the interests of American companies.

CBP Officers examine crew and passenger lists, sometimes in cooperation with the police or security personnel from federal government agencies, who may be searching for criminals or terrorists. They are authorized to search suspicious individuals and to arrest these offenders if necessary. They are also allowed to conduct body searches of suspected individuals to check for contraband. They check health clearances and ships' documents in an effort to prevent the spread of disease that may require quarantine.

Individual baggage declarations of international travelers also come under their scrutiny. CBP Officers who have baggage examination duties at points of entry into the United States classify purchases made abroad and, if necessary, assess and collect duties. All international travelers are allowed to bring home certain quantities of foreign purchases, such as perfume, clothing, tobacco, and liquor, without paying taxes. However, they must declare the amount and value of their purchases on a customs form. If they have made purchases above the duty-free limits, they must pay taxes. CBP Officers are prepared to advise tourists about U.S. customs regulations and allow them to change their customs declarations if necessary and pay the duty before baggage inspection. CBP Officers must be alert and observant to detect undeclared items. If any are discovered, it is up to the officer to decide whether an oversight or deliberate fraud has occurred. Sometimes the contraband is held and a hearing is scheduled to decide the case. A person who is caught trying to avoid paying duty is fined. When customs violations occur, officers must file detailed reports and often later appear as witnesses in court.

CBP Agriculture Specialists inspect agricultural and related goods that are imported into the United States. They act as agricultural experts at ports of entry to help protect people from agroterrorism and bioterrorism, as well as monitor agricultural imports for diseases and harmful pests.

CBP Officers and CBP Agriculture Specialists cooperate with special agents for the Federal Bureau of Investigation (FBI), the Drug Enforcement Administration, the Food and Drug Administration, and other government agencies.

Some other specialized careers in the Bureau of Customs and Border Protection are as follows:

Customs pilots, who must have a current Federal Aviation Administration (FAA) commercial pilot's license, conduct air surveillance of illegal traffic crossing U.S. borders by air, land, or sea. They apprehend, arrest, and search violators and prepare reports that are used to prosecute the criminals. They are stationed along the Canadian and Mexican borders as well as along coastal areas, flying single- and multiengine planes and helicopters.

Canine enforcement officers train and use dogs to prevent smuggling of all controlled substances as defined by customs laws. These controlled substances include marijuana, narcotics, and dangerous drugs. After undergoing an intensive 15-week basic training course in the National Detector Dog Training Center, where each officer is paired with a dog and assigned to a post, canine enforcement officers work in cooperation with CBP Officers to find and seize contraband and arrest smugglers. Canine enforcement officers also use dogs to detect bomb-making materials or other dangerous substances.

Import specialists become technical experts in a particular line of merchandise, such as wine or electronic equipment. They keep up-to-date on their area of specialization by going to trade shows and importers' places of business. Merchandise for delivery to commercial importers is examined, classified, and appraised by these specialists who must enforce import quotas and trademark laws. They use import quotas and current market values to determine the unit value of the merchandise in order to calculate the amount of money due the government in tariffs. Import specialists routinely question importers, check their lists, and make sure the merchandise matches the description and the list. If they find a violation, they call for a formal inquiry by customs special agents. Import specialists regularly deal with problems of fraud and violations of copyright and trademark laws. If the importer meets federal requirements, the import specialist issues a permit that authorizes the release of merchandise for delivery. If not, the goods might be seized and sold at public auction. These specialists encourage international trade by authorizing the lowest allowable duties on merchandise.

Customs and Border Protection chemists form a subgroup of import specialists who protect the health and safety of Americans. They analyze imported merchandise for textile fibers, lead content, narcotics, and presence of explosives or other harmful material. In many cases, the duty collected on imported products depends on the chemist's analysis and subsequent report. Customs chemists often serve as expert witnesses in court. Customs laboratories have specialized instruments that can analyze materials for their chemical components. These machines can determine such things as the amount of sucrose in a beverage, the fiber content of a textile product, the lead oxide content of fine crystal, or the presence of toxic chemicals and prohibited additives.

Criminal investigators, or *special agents,* are plainclothes investigators who make sure that the government obtains revenue on imports and that contraband and controlled substances do not enter or leave the country illegally. They investigate smuggling, criminal fraud, and major cargo thefts. Special agents target professional criminals as well as ordinary tourists who give false information on baggage declarations. Often working undercover, they cooperate with CBP Officers and the FBI. Allowed special powers of entry, search, seizure, and arrest, special agents have the broadest powers of search of any law enforcement personnel in the United States. For instance, special agents do not need probable cause or a warrant to justify search or seizure near a border or port of entry. However, in the interior of the United States, probable cause but not a warrant is necessary to conduct a search.

REQUIREMENTS

High School

If you are interested in working for the U.S. Bureau of Customs and Border Protection, you should pursue a well-rounded education in high school. Courses in government, geography and social studies, English, and history will contribute to your understanding of international and domestic legal issues as well as give you a good general background. If you wish to become a specialist in scientific or investigative aspects of the CBP, courses in the sciences, particularly chemistry, will be necessary and courses in computer science will be helpful. Taking a foreign language, especially Spanish, will also help prepare you for this career.

Postsecondary Training

Applicants to CBP must be U.S. citizens and at least 21 years of age. They must have earned at least a high school diploma, but applicants with college degrees are preferred. Applicants are required to have three years of general work experience involving contact with the public or four years of college.

Like all federal employees, applicants to CBP must pass a physical examination, undergo a security check, and pass a written test. Entrance-level appointments are at grades GS-5 and GS-7, depending on the level of education or work experience.

New CBP Officers participate in a rigorous training program that includes 10 days of pre-Academy orientation; 12 weeks of basic training at the U.S. Customs Explorer Academy; In-Port Training (a combination of on-the-job, computer-based, and classroom training); and Advanced Proficiency Training. CBP Agricultural Specialists receive specialized training from the U.S. Department of Agriculture.

Other Requirements

Applicants must be in good physical condition, possess emotional and mental stability, and demonstrate the ability to correctly apply regulations or instructional material and make clear, concise oral or written reports.

EXPLORING

There are several ways for you to learn about the various positions available at CBP. You can read *CBP Today* (http://www.customs. ustreas.gov/xp/cgov/toolbox/publications), the official employee newsletter of the United States Bureau of Customs and Border Protection, to learn more about customs work. You can also talk with people employed as customs workers, consult your high school counselors, or contact local labor union organizations and offices for additional information. Information on federal government jobs is available from offices of the state employment service, area offices of the U.S. Office of Personnel Management, and Federal Job Information Centers throughout the country.

Another great way to learn more about this career is to participate in the CBP Explorer Program. CBP Explorers receive practical and hands-on training in law enforcement and criminal justice fields. Applicants must be between the ages of 14 and 21 and have at least a C grade point average in high school or college. Participation in this program is also an excellent starting point for entry into the

Did You Know?

On a typical day in 2006, U.S. Customs and Border officials:

- Managed 326 ports of entry.

- Protected 5,000 miles of border with Canada, 1,900 miles of border with Mexico, and 95,000 miles of shoreline.

- Deployed 8,075 vehicles, 260 aircraft, 215 watercraft, and 202 equestrian patrols.

- Processed 1,100,000 passengers and pedestrians.

- Processed 70,900 truck, rail, and sea containers.

- Executed 63 arrests at ports of entry.

- Seized 1,769 pounds of narcotics in 63 seizures at ports of entry.

- Intercepted 71 fraudulent documents.

- Intercepted 20 smuggled aliens.

Source: U.S. Customs and Border Protection

field. After one year in the program, Explorers can apply to the U.S. Customs Explorer Academy.

EMPLOYERS

The U.S. Customs Service is the sole employer of customs officials. More than 40,000 customs officials are employed in the United States.

STARTING OUT

Applicants may enter the various occupations of the Bureau of Customs and Border Protection by applying to take the appropriate civil service examinations. Interested applicants should note the age, citizenship, and experience requirements previously described and realize that they will undergo a background check and a drug test. If hired, applicants will receive exacting, on-the-job training.

ADVANCEMENT

All customs agents have the opportunity to advance through a special system of promotion from within. Although they enter at the

GS-5 or GS-7 level, after one year they may compete for promotion to supervisory positions or simply to positions at a higher grade level in the agency. The journeyman level is grade GS-11. Supervisory positions at GS-12 and above are available on a competitive basis. After attaining permanent status (i.e., serving for one year on probation), customs patrol officers may compete to become special agents. Entry-level appointments for customs chemists are made at GS-5. However, applicants with advanced degrees or professional experience in the sciences, or both, should qualify for higher graded positions. Advancement potential exists for the journeyman level at GS-11 and to specialist, supervisory, and management positions at grades GS-12 and above.

EARNINGS

Entry-level positions at GS-5 began at a base annual pay of $25,195 in 2006, and entry at GS-7 started at $31,209 per year. Most CBP Officers are at the GS-11 position, which had a base annual salary of $46,189 in 2006. Supervisory positions beginning at GS-12 started at $55,360 in 2006. Federal employees in certain cities receive locality pay in addition to their salaries in order to offset the higher cost of living in those areas. Locality pay generally adds from 8.64 percent to 19.04 percent to the base salary. Certain CBP workers are also entitled to receive Law Enforcement Availability Pay, which adds another 25 percent to their salaries. All federal workers receive annual cost-of-living salary increases. Federal workers enjoy generous benefits, including health and life insurance, pension plans, and holiday, sick leave, and vacation pay.

WORK ENVIRONMENT

The customs territory of the United States is divided into nine regions that include the 50 states, the District of Columbia, Puerto Rico, and the U.S. Virgin Islands. In these regions there are some 326 ports of entry along land and sea borders. Customs inspectors may be assigned to any of these ports or to overseas work at airports, seaports, waterfronts, border stations, customs houses, or the U.S. Bureau of Customs and Border Protection Headquarters in Washington, D.C. They are able to request assignments in certain localities and usually receive them when possible.

A typical work schedule is eight hours a day, five days a week, but CBP Officers and related employees often work overtime or long into the night. United States entry and exit points must be supervised 24 hours a day, which means that workers rotate night shifts and weekend duty. CBP Officers are sometimes assigned to one-person border points at remote locations, where they may perform immigration and agricultural inspections in addition to regular duties. They often risk physical injury from criminals violating customs regulations.

OUTLOOK

Employment at the Bureau of Customs and Border Protection is steady work that is not affected by changes in the economy. With the increased emphasis on law enforcement, especially the deterrence of terrorism, but also the detection of illegally imported drugs and pornography and the prevention of exports of sensitive high-technology items, the prospects for steady employment in the CBP are likely to grow and remain high. The U.S. Department of Labor predicts employment for police and detectives, a category including CBP Officers, to grow as fast as the average through 2014.

FOR MORE INFORMATION

For career information and to view a short video about CBP Officers, visit the CBP Web site:
　　U.S. Customs and Border Protection (CBP)
　　Department of Homeland Security
　　1300 Pennsylvania Avenue, NW
　　Washington, DC 20229-0001
　　Tel: 202-354-1000
　　http://www.customs.ustreas.gov

Deputy U.S. Marshals

OVERVIEW

The United States Marshals Service forms a central part of the federal government's law enforcement efforts. As a bureau within the Department of Justice, the Marshals Service reports to the U.S. Attorney General. Among the responsibilities of *deputy U.S. marshals* are providing court security, which includes personal protection of judges, judicial officials, and jurors; serving warrants and process documents; locating and apprehending fugitives; transporting prisoners; managing the federal Witness Security Program; seizing assets used in or resulting from criminal activity; and handling special assignments and operations. There are approximately 3,065 deputy U.S. marshals employed throughout the United States.

HISTORY

The U.S. Marshals Service has its roots in the Judiciary Act, passed by Congress in 1789, which established not only the post of U.S. marshal but also the country's original federal court system. The act delegated two duties to the marshals: to enforce all precepts issued by the federal government and to protect and attend to the federal courts. Marshals were also authorized to hire one or more deputies.

The U.S. Senate confirmed the first 13 U.S. marshals, appointed by President George Washington, on September 26, 1789. Over the next year, two more marshals were chosen. The 13 original states, as well as the districts of Kentucky and Maine, were each assigned a marshal to represent the federal governments interests at a local level. The number of marshals and deputies increased as the United States

QUICK FACTS

School Subjects
Computer science
Foreign language
Government

Personal Skills
Helping/teaching
Leadership/management

Work Environment
Indoors and outdoors
Primarily multiple locations

Minimum Education Level
High school diploma

Salary Range
$25,195 to $31,209 to $118,957

Certification or Licensing
None available

Outlook
Faster than the average

DOT
377

GOE
04.03.01

NOC
N/A

O*NET-SOC
N/A

expanded westward, and with a rise in the country's population, some states were assigned more than one marshal. By the 2000s, there were approximately 3,065 deputy U.S. marshals assigned to the 94 federal judicial districts across the United States and Puerto Rico, Guam, the Virgin Islands, and the Northern Marianas.

The duties of the Marshals Service expanded soon after the appointment of the first marshals. Marshals and deputies were required, for example, to play a major role in taking the national census (a responsibility that lasted until 1870), to supervise federal penitentiaries in the western territories, to enforce precepts from the French consuls, to take custody of goods seized by customs officers, and to sell seized lands. Along with the increase in responsibilities came a corresponding growth in the number of superiors to whom the Marshals Service was accountable. By the mid-19th century, the federal courts, the Secretary of the Treasury, the Solicitor of the Treasury, and the Secretary of the Interior all had supervisory powers over some aspects of the work of the marshals and deputies. In 1861, however, the Marshals Service came under the exclusive power of the attorney general, and in 1870 the service became a part of the newly created Department of Justice.

U.S. marshals and their deputies have frequently faced potentially dangerous situations. The level of danger was especially great in the 19th century for those who were charged with keeping order in newly established western territories. During the Oklahoma land rush, for example, more than 60 marshals were killed in a span of just five years. It is the Marshals Service of the late 19th century—the time of legendary marshals Bat Masterson and Wyatt Earp—that is dramatized in numerous books and films about the role of marshals and deputies in the Old West. Some might also remember that marshals and deputies were charged with quelling civil disturbances such as the Whiskey Rebellion of 1791, the Pullman Strike of 1894, and the antiwar protests of the late 1960s; enforcing school integration beginning in the 1960s; and confronting militant Native Americans at Wounded Knee, South Dakota, in 1973. Today, the men and women of the Marshals Service, trained in the latest techniques and equipment, continue to perform a wide variety of law enforcement and homeland security duties under the attorney general and the U.S. Department of Justice.

THE JOB

One of the oldest duties of the U.S. Marshals Service is court security. Originally, this entailed the presence of a marshal or deputy in the courtroom to maintain order and to ensure the safety of the judge. In time, however, the job of protecting the courts has become much more complex. Now, depending on the trial, prosecutors, attorneys, jurors, witnesses, family members, and any other trial participant potentially in danger might be provided with security. Marshals have been assisted in carrying out these responsibilities by using advanced equipment—high-tech alarm systems, for example—as well as by improved law enforcement techniques. The Marshals Service is sometimes alerted to dangers by threats mentioned in letters or phone calls or by informants, but deputies cannot rely on these explicit means of warning. Constant vigilance is required.

A special area related to court security is the federal Witness Security Program. Witnesses who risk their lives to testify against organized crime figures or others involved in major criminal activity are given around-the-clock protection. After the trial, the witnesses are relocated to another part of the country and given a new identity. The Marshals Service provides support programs to help these witnesses adjust to their new identities and environments.

A significant part of the workload involves serving process documents and executing court orders. Private process-serving companies work for the courts to serve papers for civil cases, but the Marshals Service handles almost all of the criminal process-serving needs of the court. There are many kinds of process documents, including subpoenas, restraining orders, notices of condemnations, and summonses. In the days of the Old West, serving process documents was one of their most dangerous duties, sometimes entailing traveling on horseback for long distances, as well as face-to-face shootouts. Sophisticated equipment, allowing for better means of surveillance and coordination, has made this task less threatening. The Marshals Service now handles about one million process documents each year.

Even more dangerous are the execution of arrest warrants and the apprehension of fugitives. Along with other federal agencies, such as the Federal Bureau of Investigation (FBI), the Marshals Service continues to perform these tasks, handling more than 44,000 arrest warrants each year and apprehending more fugitives than all other federal law enforcement agencies combined. The Marshals Service is responsible for locating and apprehending many types of fugitives, including parole and probation violators and prisoners who have escaped from federal prisons.

For most of its history, the Marshals Service has been charged with the responsibility of seizing, managing, and disposing of property involved in criminal cases. Many of these cases now involve drug trafficking. Planes, cars, boats, houses and condominiums, ranches, businesses, and restaurants, as well as personal assets such as jewelry and cash, are some examples of the type of property seized. Property seized in this manner is forfeited under the law and then sold off at public auctions or by other means. Seized property may also be transferred to law enforcement agencies for official use.

The Marshals Service is also in charge of transporting federal prisoners. Using automobiles, buses, vans, and aircraft—some of them obtained by the asset seizure program—U.S. Marshals supervise the movements of more than 300,000 prisoners each year. After a trial, convicts awaiting a sentence are also the responsibility of the Marshals Service. The average number of prisoners held in custody each day by the Marshals Service is approximately 54,000.

Protecting the shipment of weapons systems is a more recent responsibility. Under an agreement with the United States Air Force, deputies direct traffic and help escort vehicles transporting weapons systems, deterring or arresting anyone who attempts to disrupt the shipment.

Within the Marshals Service is a rapid-deployment force called the Special Operations Group (SOG). The unit was formed in 1971 in order to handle national emergencies, such as civil disturbances, hostage cases, or terrorist attacks. Members of SOG are regular deputies, located in all parts of the country, who are given specialized training and who must always be on call for emergencies.

REQUIREMENTS

High School

If you are interested in becoming a deputy U.S. marshal, you must complete high school and obtain an undergraduate degree or equivalent experience. In high school, you should pursue a general course of study that includes courses in government, one or more foreign languages, English, history, and computer science.

Postsecondary Training

The Marshals Service requires that candidates have a minimum level of education or experience. A four-year bachelor's degree in any major is sufficient. Without an undergraduate degree, however, an applicant needs at least three years' experience in a job demonstrating poise and self-confidence under stress, as well as the ability to reason soundly, make decisions quickly, find practical solutions, accept responsibility, interact tactfully with a wide range of people, and prepare reports. Although any number of occupations may fulfill these requirements, the following are examples of acceptable experience: (1) law enforcement; (2) correctional treatment and supervision of inmates; (3) classroom teaching; (4) volunteer work or counseling for a community action program; (5) sales work (but not over-the-counter sales positions); (6) interviewing; or (7) jobs, such as a credit rating investigator, claims adjuster, or journalist, that require public contact for the purpose of collecting information. For candidates who have been to college but do not have a degree, every year of study is accepted as nine months of experience.

All candidates are required to take a written test of 125 questions. A score of 78 or better is passing. The questions are intended to evaluate clerical skills, the ability to reason verbally, and the level of proficiency in abstract reasoning (that is, using symbols and numbers). Candidates are also given a personal interview and, as for all government jobs, must be willing to undergo an extensive background check.

Once hired, new deputy marshals are sent to a 10-week basic training program at the U.S. Marshals Service Training Academy in Glynco, Georgia. The program features courses in law enforcement, criminal investigation, forensics, and areas particular to the Marshals Service. There are also a rigorous physical fitness program and 18 months of on-the-job training.

Other Requirements

Before being hired, candidates must pass a background investigation, drug test, and medical examination. They must also be U.S. citizens who are between the ages of 21 and 36. Like those in other law enforcement positions, deputy U.S. marshals must be in excellent physical shape, and must pass a Fitness-In-Total assessment. Moreover, their vision must be no worse than 20/200 uncorrected in both eyes (corrected to at least 20/20); they must have good hearing (equivalent to being able to hear a whispered voice at 15 feet); and they may not have insulin-dependent diabetes or any other health condition that might interfere with job performance or endanger the health and safety of others.

EXPLORING

For any law enforcement job, it is difficult to obtain practical experience prior to entering the field. If you are interested in more information about working as a deputy U.S. marshal, you should write directly to the Marshals Service. Many police departments, however, hire student trainees and interns, and this may provide good exposure to general law enforcement. In addition, the FBI operates an Honors Internship Program (https://www.fbijobs.gov/231.asp) for undergraduate and graduate students selected by the FBI. A school guidance counselor, a college or university career services office, or a public library may also have additional information.

EMPLOYERS

The U.S. Marshals Service is the sole employer of the approximately 3,067 deputy U.S. marshals.

STARTING OUT

The Marshals Service accepts only candidates who have fulfilled the necessary physical, educational, and experiential requirements listed above. Those interested in pursuing the field should contact the Marshals Service to find out when and where the written examination will take place.

Candidates with postsecondary education, particularly undergraduate and graduate degrees in fields related to law, law enforcement, criminology, or political science, will have the strongest chance of joining the U.S. Marshals Service. Knowledge of foreign languages, and specialized skills, including computer and electronics skills, are also in high demand by the U.S. Marshals office.

ADVANCEMENT

Advancement is made on the basis of merit and experience. Within a district office, the top position is that of U.S. marshal. Appointed by the president of the United States, U.S. marshals must be confirmed by the U.S. Senate. Directly under the U.S. Marshal is the *Chief Deputy U.S. Marshal,* who oversees the district's staff of supervisors, the deputy U.S. marshals, and the support staff. Each district also employs specialists in witness security, court security, and seized property.

EARNINGS

As with other federal positions, salaries for deputy U.S. marshals are fixed at government service rating levels. Beginning deputy U.S. marshals are generally hired at the GS-5 level, at which an annual salary was between $25,195 and $32,755 in 2006. Deputy U.S.

marshals with bachelor's and especially advanced degrees in law enforcement, criminology, law, and other related disciplines may be hired at the GS-7 level, which draws a salary between $31,209 and $40,569. Those appointed at the GS-5 grade level are eligible for promotion to GS-7 after one year, and those appointed at the GS-7 grade level are eligible for promotion to GS-9 after one year.

Top salaries for deputy U.S. marshals are at the GS-11 level, which paid a base rate of $46,189 per year in 2006, but deputy U.S. marshals certified in a specialty area may earn the GS-12 level, which was $55,360 in 2006. The top rating, GS-15, paid $91,507 to $118,957 per year in 2006.

In addition, deputies assigned to certain cities—including New York; Los Angeles; Boston; Miami; San Francisco; Washington, D.C.; Alexandria, Va.; and others—receive higher pay based on the higher cost of living in these areas. All federal workers receive annual cost-of-living salary increases.

Benefits include health and life insurance, paid vacations and holidays, and a pension program. Most federal law enforcement officials are eligible for early retirement.

WORK ENVIRONMENT

In general, deputy U.S. marshals work 40 hours a week. These hours are usually during the daytime, Monday through Friday, but overtime and other shifts are sometimes required. Travel may be necessary, for example, to transport a prisoner from one state to another.

Deputies generally work out of well-maintained, clean offices, but their duties can take them to a wide variety of environments, such as a courtroom; an automobile, helicopter, or airplane; the streets of a major U.S. city; or, when trying to locate a fugitive, a foreign country.

Like all law enforcement jobs, personal safety is a concern. Those interested in working for the U.S. Marshals Service should be well aware of the potential for physical harm or even death. Because of the danger, deputies carry firearms and are well trained in self-defense and other paramilitary techniques. Strenuous physical exertion, emotional stress, and exposure to harsh conditions (such as poor weather) are often a part of the job.

For some deputies, an advantage of the job is the diversity of cases. Others find personal satisfaction in knowing that they are serving their country. Deputy U.S. marshals enjoy great respect and confidence from the public.

OUTLOOK

There are close to 3,067 deputy U.S. marshals assigned to the 94 districts across the United States and Puerto Rico, Guam, the Virgin Islands, and the Northern Marianas. Changes in the service's budget, as well as increases or decreases in the responsibilities assigned the service, affect employment opportunities. Careers in law enforcement and security-related fields in general are expected to grow rapidly in some cases, as federal and state governments pass new "tough-on-crime" legislation and the number of criminals continues to grow. Great increases in the crime rate will most likely prompt public pressures to increase hiring of law enforcement officials, including deputy U.S. marshals. Threats of terrorist activity have put all public safety officials on alert, from FBI and CIA experts to local police forces and private security companies. There is now increased security particularly in and around government offices, public buildings, airports, post offices, and media headquarters.

In spite of the continuing need for deputy U.S. marshals, competition for available positions will remain high because of the prestige offered by this career and the generous benefits available to many careers in federal service.

FOR MORE INFORMATION

For information on career opportunities, contact
U.S. Marshals Service
Human Resources Division—Law Enforcement Recruiting
Washington, DC 20530-1000
Tel: 202-307-9400
Email: us.marshals@usdoj.gov
http://www.usdoj.gov/marshals

Detectives

OVERVIEW

Detectives are almost always plainclothes investigators who gather difficult-to-obtain information on criminal activity and other subjects. They conduct interviews and surveillance, locate missing persons and criminal suspects, examine records, and write detailed reports. Some make arrests and take part in raids.

HISTORY

The United States inherited much of its law enforcement tradition from England. During the early history of the United States, bounty hunters (sometimes called stipendiary police or thieftakers) usually handled criminal investigation. Governments, private individuals, or businesses (such as insurance companies) paid these early detectives a reward or fee for apprehending suspected criminals or returning stolen property. Many bounty hunters were petty criminals themselves.

The early 19th century saw growing social unrest and criminal activity in the United States, as the country moved from an agrarian to an industrialized, urban economy. By the mid-1800s, the upsurge in crime led to public calls for greater government action. The first police department in the United States was formed in New York City in 1844. Before long many cities and towns across the country also established organized police forces, including special investigative divisions. The investigation of crimes, however, was still commonly handled by stipendiary

QUICK FACTS

School Subjects
English
Government
History

Personal Skills
Leadership/management
Technical/scientific

Work Environment
Indoors and outdoors
One location with some
  travel

Minimum Education Level
High school diploma

Salary Range
$19,230 to $55,720 to
  $88,570+

Certification or Licensing
Voluntary (certification)
Required by certain states
  (licensing)

Outlook
About as fast as the average
  (police detectives)
Faster than the average
  (private detectives)

DOT
375

GOE
04.03.01

NOC
6261

O*NET-SOC
33-3021.00, 33-3021.01,
  33-9021.00

police and thieftakers. Although police departments were created with the hope of reducing crime, numerous scandals within their own ranks soon erupted. Corruption within local police departments was a continual problem and, by the early 1900s, became a motivating cause for police reforms and for the establishment of state police agencies, including state investigative divisions.

Also notable during the 19th century was the growth of private investigative firms. The Pinkerton National Detective Agency, formed by Allan Pinkerton in the early 1850s, was probably the most famous, namely for its ability to apprehend train robbers, kidnappers, thieves, and forgers. The company's reputation, along with Pinkerton's rejection of rewards in favor of a set daily fee for his agents, helped establish professional standards for detective work.

In 1865, the U.S. Secret Service was formed. Although later associated with the protection of the president and other officials, the secret service was created to investigate counterfeit money. Another federal agency, the Bureau of Investigation (later the Federal Bureau of Investigation, or FBI), was created in 1908 by executive order of President Theodore Roosevelt. It began by investigating criminal activity on government property, crimes by government officials, antitrust cases, and numerous fraudulent schemes.

In the 20th century, the federal government established a number of other investigative agencies. During Prohibition, thousands of detectives were employed by the Treasury Department to enforce the government's ban on alcoholic beverages as well as to investigate the escalating crime surrounding the sale of liquor. Today narcotics squad detectives, employed by the U.S. Drug Enforcement Administration, are charged with a similar duty.

Advances in technology have revolutionized the field of criminal investigation. Fingerprinting, which police departments started using widely in the early 1900s, had a great impact on the identification and detection of criminals. Methods of analyzing bloodstains, saliva, and hair and skin traces, as well as precise ways of matching up various inorganic substances, such as paint and cloth fibers, have also aided detectives. More recently, voiceprinting and the genetic technique of DNA-printing have shown promise for more sophisticated detection.

THE JOB

The job of a *police detective* begins after a crime has been committed. Uniformed police officers are usually the first to be dispatched to the scene of a crime, however, and it is police officers who are generally required to fill out the initial crime report. A detective often begins an investigation with this report.

Detectives may also receive help early on from other members of the police department. Evidence technicians are sometimes sent immediately to the scene of a crime to comb the area for physical evidence. This step is important because most crime scenes contain physical evidence that could link a suspect to the crime. Fingerprints are the most common physical piece of evidence, but other clues, such as broken locks, broken glass, and footprints, as well as blood, skin, or hair traces, are also useful. If there is a suspect on the scene, torn clothing or any scratches, cuts, and bruises are noted. Specially trained crime lab technicians may then test the physical evidence.

It is after this initial stage that the case is assigned to a police detective. Police detectives may be assigned as many as two or three cases a day, and having 30 cases to handle at one time is not unusual. Because there is only a limited amount of time, an important part of a detective's work is to determine which cases have the greatest chance of being solved. The most serious offenses or those in which there is considerable evidence and obvious leads tend to receive the highest priority. All cases, however, are given at least a routine follow-up investigation.

Police detectives have numerous means of gathering additional information. For example, they contact and interview victims and witnesses, familiarize themselves with the scene of the crime and places where a suspect may spend time, and conduct surveillance operations. Detectives sometimes have informers who provide important leads. Because detectives must often work undercover, they wear ordinary clothes, not police uniforms. Also helpful are existing police files on other crimes, on known criminals, and on people suspected of criminal activity. If sufficient evidence has been collected, the police detective will arrest the suspect, sometimes with the help of uniformed police officers.

Once the suspect is in custody, it is the job of the police detective to conduct an interrogation. Questioning the suspect may reveal new evidence and help determine whether the suspect was involved in other unsolved crimes. Before finishing the case, the detective must prepare a detailed written report. Detectives are sometimes required to present evidence at the trial of the suspect.

Criminal investigation is just one area in which *private investigators* are involved. Some specialize, for example, in finding missing persons, while others may investigate insurance fraud, gather information on the background of persons involved in divorce or child custody cases, administer lie detection tests, debug offices and telephones, or offer security services. Cameras, video equipment, tape recorders, and lock picks are used in compliance with legal restrictions to obtain necessary information. Some private investigators work for themselves, but many others work for detective agencies or businesses. Clients include private individuals, corporations concerned with theft, insurance companies suspicious of fraud, and lawyers who want information for a case. Whoever the client, the private investigator is usually expected to provide a detailed report of the activities and results of the investigation.

REQUIREMENTS

High School

Because detectives work on a wide variety of cases, if you are interested in this field, you are encouraged to take a diverse course load. English, American history, business law, government, psychology, sociology, chemistry, and physics are suggested, as are courses in journalism, computers, and a foreign language. The ability to type is often needed. To become a police detective, you must first have experience as a police officer. Hiring requirements for police officers vary, but most departments require at least a high school diploma.

Postsecondary Training

In some police departments, a college degree may be necessary for some or all positions. Many colleges and universities offer courses

Learn More About It

Brown, Steven Kerry. *The Complete Idiot's Guide to Private Investigating.* 2d ed. Royersford, Penn.: Alpha, 2007.

Cooper, Chris. *Behind the Private Eye: Surveillance Tales & Techniques.* Seattle, Wash.: BookSurge Publishing, 2005.

Harrison, Wayne. *PI School: How To Become A Private Detective.* Boulder, Colo.: Paladin Press, 1991.

Sennewald, Charles, and John Tsukayama. *The Process of Investigation.* 3d ed. Woburn, Mass.: Butterworth-Heinemann, 2006.

Tillman, Norma M. *Private Investigation 101.* Nashville, Tenn.: Norma Tillman Enterprises, 2006.

or programs in police science, criminal justice, or law enforcement. Newly hired police officers are generally sent to a police academy for job training.

After gaining substantial experience in the department—usually about three to five years—and demonstrating the skills required for detective work, a police officer may be promoted to detective. In some police departments, candidates must first take a qualifying exam. For new detectives, there is usually a training program, which may last from a few weeks to several months.

Private detective agencies usually do not hire individuals without previous experience. A large number of private investigators are former police officers. Those with no law enforcement experience who want to become private investigators can enroll in special private investigation schools, although these do not guarantee qualification for employment. A college degree is an admissions requirement at some private investigation schools. These schools teach skills essential to detective work, such as how to take and develop fingerprints, pick locks, test for the presence of human blood, investigate robberies, identify weapons, and take photographs. The length of these programs and their admissions requirements vary considerably. Some are correspondence programs, while others offer classroom instruction and an internship at a detective agency. Experience can also be gained by taking classes in law enforcement, police science, or criminal justice at a college or university.

Certification or Licensing

The National Association of Legal Investigators awards the certified legal investigator designation to private detectives and investigators who specialize in cases that deal with negligence or criminal defense investigations.

Private detectives and investigators must be licensed in all states except for Alabama, Alaska, Colorado, Idaho, Mississippi, Missouri, and South Dakota. In general, states that have licensing require applicants to pass a written examination and file a bond. Depending on the state, applicants may also need to have a minimum amount of experience, either as a police officer or as an apprentice under a licensed private investigator. An additional license is sometimes required for carrying a gun.

In almost all large cities, the hiring of police officers must follow local civil service regulations. In such cases, candidates generally must be at least 21 years old, U.S. citizens, and within the locally prescribed height and weight limits. Other requirements include 20/20 corrected vision and good hearing. Background checks are often done.

The civil service board usually gives both a written and physical examination. The written test is intended to measure a candidate's mental aptitude for police work, while the physical examination focuses on strength, dexterity, and agility.

Other Requirements
Among the most important personal characteristics helpful for detectives are an inquisitive mind, good observation skills, a keen memory, and well-developed oral and written communication skills. The large amount of physical activity involved requires that detectives be in good shape. An excellent moral character is especially important.

EXPLORING

There are few means of exploring the field of detective work, and actual experience in the field prior to employment is unlikely. Some police departments, however, do hire teenagers for positions as police trainees and interns. If you are interested in becoming a detective, you should talk with your school guidance counselor, your local police department, local private detective agencies, a private investigation school, or a college or university offering police science, criminal justice, or law enforcement courses. In addition, the FBI operates an Honors Internship Program for undergraduate and graduate students that exposes interns to a variety of investigative techniques.

EMPLOYERS

There are more than 842,000 police and detectives in the United States. A large percentage work for police departments or other government agencies. In 2004, approximately 43,000 detectives worked as private investigators, employed either for themselves, for a private detective firm, or for a business.

STARTING OUT

If you are interested in becoming a detective, you should contact your local police department, the civil service office or examining board, or private detective agencies in your area to determine hiring practices and any special requirements. Newspapers may list available jobs. If you earn a college degree in police science, criminal justice, or law enforcement, you may benefit from your institution's career services or guidance office. Some police academies accept candidates not sponsored by a police department, and for some people this may be the best way to enter police work.

ADVANCEMENT

Advancement within a police department may depend on several factors, such as job performance, length of service, formal education and training courses, and special examinations. Large city police departments, divided into separate divisions with their own administrations, often provide greater advancement possibilities.

Because of the high dropout rate for private investigators, those who manage to stay in the field for more than five years have an excellent chance for advancement. Supervisory and management positions exist, and some private investigators start their own agencies.

EARNINGS

Median annual earnings of police detectives and criminal investigators were $55,790 in 2005, according to the U.S. Department of Labor. The lowest 10 percent earned $32,920 or less, while the highest 10 percent earned more than $88,570 annually. Median annual earnings were $75,700 in federal government, $48,680 in state government, and $53,820 in local government. Compensation generally increases considerably with experience. Police departments generally offer better than average benefits, including health insurance, paid vacation, sick days, and pension plans.

Median annual earnings of salaried private detectives and investigators were $32,650 in 2005, according to the U.S. Department of Labor. The lowest 10 percent earned less than $19,230, and the highest 10 percent earned more than $61,520.

Private investigators who are self-employed have the potential for making much higher salaries. Hourly fees of $50 to $150 and even more, excluding expenses, are possible. Detectives who work for an agency may receive benefits, such as health insurance, but self-employed investigators must provide their own.

WORK ENVIRONMENT

The working conditions of a detective are diverse. Almost all of them work out of an office, where they may consult with colleagues, interview witnesses, read documents, or contact people on the telephone.

Their assignments bring detectives to a wide range of environments. Interviews at homes or businesses may be necessary. Traveling is also common. Rarely do jobs expose a detective to possible physical harm or death, but detectives are more likely than most people to place themselves in a dangerous situation.

Schedules for detectives are often irregular, and overtime, as well as night and weekend hours, may be necessary. At some police departments and detective agencies, overtime is compensated with additional pay or time off.

Although the work of a detective is portrayed as exciting in popular culture, the job has its share of monotonous and discouraging moments. For example, detectives may need to sit in a car for many hours waiting for a suspect to leave a building entrance only to find that the suspect is not there. Even so, the great variety of cases usually makes the work interesting.

OUTLOOK

Employment for police detectives is expected to increase about as fast as the average for all other occupations through 2014, according to the U.S. Department of Labor. Many openings will likely result from police detectives retiring or leaving their departments for other reasons.

Employment for private investigators is predicted to grow faster than the average through 2014, although it is important to keep in mind that law enforcement or comparable experience is often required for employment. The use of private investigators by insurance firms, restaurants, hotels, and other businesses is on the rise. Two areas of particular growth are the investigation of the various forms of computer fraud and the conducting of employee background checks.

FOR MORE INFORMATION

Contact the IACP for information about careers in law enforcement.
International Association of Chiefs of Police (IACP)
515 North Washington Street
Alexandria, VA 22314-2357
Tel: 703-836-6767
Email: information@theiacp.org
http://www.theiacp.org

For more information on private investigation, contact
National Association of Investigative Specialists
PO Box 82148
Austin, TX 78708-2148
Tel: 512-719-3595
http://www.pimall.com/nais/nais.j.html

For information on certification, contact
National Association of Legal Investigators
c/o Alan E. Goodman, National Director
PO Box 8479
Portland, ME 04104-8479
Tel: 888-244-5685
Email: info@nalionline.org
http://www.nalionline.org

FBI Agents

QUICK FACTS

School Subjects
English
Foreign language
Government

Personal Skills
Communication/ideas
Leadership/management

Work Environment
Indoors and outdoors
Primarily multiple locations

Minimum Education Level
Bachelor's degree

Salary Range
$42,040 to $65,832 to
$100,000+

Certification or Licensing
None available

Outlook
About as fast as the average

DOT
375

GOE
04.03.01

NOC
N/A

O*NET-SOC
N/A

OVERVIEW

FBI agents, special agents of the Federal Bureau of Investigation (FBI), are employees of the federal government. The FBI is responsible for investigating and enforcing more than 200 federal statutes that encompass terrorism, organized crime, white-collar crime, public corruption, financial crime, government fraud, bribery, copyright matters, civil rights violations, bank robbery, extortion, kidnapping, air piracy, terrorism, foreign counterintelligence, interstate criminal activity, and fugitive and drug trafficking matters. Agents also conduct background investigations on certain federal government job applicants. There are approximately 11,660 FBI agents employed in the United States.

HISTORY

The Federal Bureau of Investigation was founded in 1908 as the investigative branch of the U.S. Department of Justice. In its earliest years, the FBI's responsibilities were limited. However, the creation of new federal laws gave the FBI jurisdiction over criminal matters that had previously been regulated by the individual states, such as those involving the interstate transportation of stolen vehicles. By the 1920s, the FBI was also used for political purposes, such as tracking down alleged subversive elements and spying on political enemies.

Early in its history, the FBI developed a reputation for corruption. In 1924, J. Edgar Hoover was appointed as director of the Bureau and charged with the twin goals of cleaning up the agency and making the agency's work independent from politics. Hoover established stricter professional standards, eliminating corruption, and, partly because of Hoover's own ambitions, the FBI's responsibilities increased. Soon the FBI was the most powerful law enforcement agency in the country.

The FBI established its identification division in 1924, and the Bureau's scientific laboratory in 1932. Then, in 1934, the FBI was given the general authority to handle federal crime investigation. Within three years, more than 11,000 federal criminals were convicted through the FBI's efforts. As its prestige grew, the FBI was further designated, in 1939, as the central clearinghouse for all matters pertaining to the internal security of the United States. During World War II, FBI agents rendered many security services for plants involved in war production and worked to gather evidence on espionage activities within the plants.

Since its inception in 1932, the FBI laboratory has become one of the largest and most comprehensive crime laboratories in the world, providing leadership and service in the scientific solution and prosecution of crimes. It is the only full-service federal forensic laboratory in the United States. As a result, today the FBI is involved in a wide variety of law enforcement activities using the latest scientific methods and forms of analysis available.

The FBI's identification division serves as the nation's repository and clearinghouse for fingerprint records. The fingerprint section of the FBI laboratory is the largest in the world, containing millions of sets of fingerprints. In this capacity, the division provides the following services: identifying and maintaining fingerprint records for arrested criminal suspects and for applicants to sensitive jobs; posting notices for people wanted for crimes and for parole or probation violations; examining physical evidence for fingerprints and providing occasional court testimony on the results of examinations; training in fingerprint science; maintaining fingerprint records of people currently reported missing; and identifying amnesia victims and unknown deceased people.

After World War II, the FBI began conducting background security investigations for government agencies, as well as probes into internal security matters for the executive branch of the federal government. The 1960s brought civil rights and organized crime to the forefront for the FBI, and the '70s and '80s focused on counterterrorism, financial crime, drugs, and violent crimes. During the 1990s, the FBI continued to focus on these crimes, as well as address the growing threat of cybercrime. The bureau created the Computer Investigations and Infrastructure Threat Assessment Center and other initiatives to respond to physical and cyber attacks against infrastructure in the United States. The FBI's mission changed as a result of the terrorist attacks of September 11, 2001. While still investigating all types of federal crime, the bureau's most important mandate today is to protect the American people from future terrorist attacks.

THE JOB

The FBI has the broadest investigative authority of all federal law enforcement agencies. The agency leads long-term, complex investigations, while working closely with other federal, state, local, and foreign law enforcement and intelligence agencies.

An FBI special agent is faced with the challenge of investigating and upholding certain federal laws that come under the FBI's jurisdictions. Throughout their career, FBI agents conduct investigations on a variety of issues that are lumped into the following categories: counterterrorism, counterintelligence, cyber investigations, public corruption, civil rights, organized crime, white-collar crime (such as antitrust investigations, bankruptcy fraud, environmental crime, financial institution fraud, government fraud, health care fraud, insurance fraud, money laundering, securities/commodities fraud, and telemarketing fraud), and major thefts/violent crimes (such as art theft, crimes against children, jewelry and gem theft, and Indian Country crime). FBI agents may be assigned to a wide range of investigations, unless they have specialized skills in a certain area. In short, agents are assigned to a case, conduct an investigation, and then submit a report of their findings to the U.S. Attorney's Office.

During an investigation, agents may use a vast network of communication systems and the bureau's crime detection laboratory to help them with their work. Agents may gather information with the help of the National Crime Information Center and the Criminal Justice Information Services Division. Once they have information, agents must make sure the facts and evidence are correct. FBI agents may discuss their findings with a U.S. attorney or an assistant U.S. attorney, who decides whether the evidence requires legal action. The Justice Department may choose to investigate the matter further, and the FBI agents may obtain a search warrant or court order to locate and seize property that may be evidence. If the Justice Department decides to prosecute the case, the agent may then obtain an arrest warrant.

With the goal of gathering information and reporting it, FBI agents may spend a considerable amount of time traveling or living in various cities. Their investigations often require the agent

FBI agents begin making sketches in the front yard of a fellow agent who was arrested for espionage after he allegedly dropped off a package of classified information at a park. *(Doug Mills/AP)*

to interview people—witnesses, subjects, or suspects—and search for different types of records. Agents may set up a stakeout to watch a place or person. Special Agents may also work with paid informants. Sometimes agents testify in court about their investigations or findings. If enough incriminating evidence is found, FBI agents conduct arrests or raids of various types. Agents must carry firearms while on duty, and they typically carry their bureau identification badge. Agents always carry their credentials. Most of the time they wear everyday business suits or other appropriate attire—not uniforms.

Some agents with specialized skills may work specific types of investigations, such as fraud or embezzlement. *Language specialists*—who can be employed as special agents or support personnel—may translate foreign language over a wiretap and tape recordings into English. The FBI also employs agents specializing in areas such as chemistry, physics, metallurgy, or computers. *Laboratory specialists* analyze physical evidence like blood, hair, and body fluids, while others analyze handwriting, documents, and firearms. Agents working for the FBI's Behavioral Science Unit track and profile serial murderers, rapists, and other criminals committing patterned violent crimes.

Agents often work alone, unless the investigation is particularly dangerous or requires more agents. However, FBI agents do not investigate local matters—only federal violations that fall within their jurisdiction. The agents' work can be discussed only with other bureau employees, which means they cannot discuss investigations with their families or friends.

The FBI operates 56 field offices, over 400 resident agencies, four specialized field installations, and 50 foreign liaison posts. FBI agents must be willing to be reassigned at any point in their career.

REQUIREMENTS

High School

A high school diploma, or its equivalent, is required. The FBI does not recommend specific courses for high school students. Rather, the bureau encourages students to do the best work they can. Since FBI agents perform a variety of work, numerous academic disciplines are needed.

Postsecondary Training

All special agent candidates must hold a four-year degree from a college or university that is accredited by one of the regional or national institutional associations recognized by the U.S. Department of Education. Candidates must fulfill additional requirements of one of four entry programs: Law, Accounting, Language, and Diversified. Entry through the law program requires a law degree from an accredited resident law school. The accounting program requires a bachelor's degree in accounting or related discipline, such as economics, business, or finance. Applicants for the accounting program must have passed the Uniform Certified Accountant Examination or at least show eligibility to take this exam. Language program applicants may hold a bachelor's degree in any discipline, but must demonstrate fluency in one or more foreign languages meeting the current needs of the FBI. In recent years, these languages have included Spanish, Arabic, Farsi, Pashtu, Urdu, Chinese, Japanese, Korean, Vietnamese, and Russian. The diversified program accepts applicants with a bachelor's degree in any discipline plus three years of full-time work experience or an advanced degree accompanied by two years of full-time work experience.

The FBI especially values applicants with law or accounting degrees. Since agents investigate violations of federal law, a law degree may give applicants an appreciation and understanding of the Federal Rules of Criminal Procedure. Plus, a law degree should help agents identify the elements of a criminal violation and collect the necessary evidence for successful prosecution. Since FBI agents trace financial transactions and review and analyze complex accounting records, an accounting degree will likely help agents document evidence and reveal sophisticated financial crimes.

All candidates must complete a rigorous application process. For those who successfully complete the written tests and interview, the FBI conducts a thorough background investigation that includes credit and criminal record checks; interviews with associates; contact with personal and business references; interviews with past employers and neighbors; and verification of educational achievements. Drug testing and a physical examination are required. A polygraph examination is also required. The completed background investigation is then considered when the final hiring decision is made.

If appointed to the position of an FBI special agent, new hires train for 18 weeks at the FBI Academy in Quantico, Virginia. Agent trainees spend a total of 708 instructional hours studying academic and investigative subjects, and trainees also focus on physical fitness, defensive tactics, and firearms training. Emphasis is placed on developing investigative techniques, as well as skills in interviewing, interrogation, and gathering intelligence information. Agent trainees are tested on their defensive tactics, firearms and weapon handling, physical fitness, and arrest techniques. They must also pass academic exams and obey certain rules and regulations during the training. If the trainees pass the tests at the academy and receive their credentials, they become special agents and are assigned to serve a two-year probationary period at an FBI field office.

After graduation from the FBI Academy, new agents are assigned to an FBI field office for a probationary period lasting one year, after which they become permanent special agents. During the first months of employment, the novice agent is guided by a veteran special agent who will help show how the lessons learned at the academy can be applied on the job. Assignments are determined by the individual's special skills and the current needs of the FBI. As a part of their duties, special agents may be required to relocate during their careers.

The education and training of FBI agents continue throughout their career. FBI agents are always expected to learn new techniques and better methods in criminal investigation, either through experience on the job, advanced study courses, in-service training, or special conferences.

Other Requirements

To qualify for training as an FBI agent, candidates must be U.S. citizens between the ages of 23 and 36. They must possess a valid driver's license, be available for assignment anywhere in the areas of the Bureau's jurisdiction, which includes Puerto Rico, and be in excellent physical condition. Their vision must not be worse than 20/200 uncorrected and correctable to 20/20 in one eye and no worse than 20/40 in the other eye. Applicants must also pass a color-vision test and hearing test. Applicants may not have physical disabilities that would interfere with the performance of their duties, including use of firearms and defensive tactics and taking part in raids. All applicants must be able to withstand rigorous physical strain and exertion.

FBI agents assume grave responsibilities as a normal part of their jobs. Their reputation, integrity, and character must be above reproach, and they must be dependable and courageous. Agents must be able to accept continual challenges in their jobs, realizing that no two days of work assignments may be exactly alike. FBI agents need to be stable and personally secure and able to work daily with challenge, change, and danger. For most agents, the FBI is a lifelong career.

EXPLORING

The best method of exploring a career with the FBI is to participate in the FBI Honors Internship Program, which is held every summer in Washington, D.C. Participation is open to undergraduate and graduate students selected by the FBI. This program is designed to give interns experience and insight into the inner workings of, and career opportunities available at, the FBI. Students are assigned to various divisions of the agency according to their academic disciplines, and they work alongside special agents under the supervision of assistant directors. Interns may work at FBI headquarters or other agency locations in the Washington, D.C., area. Acceptance into the internship program is highly competitive. Applicants must be full-time students intending to return to school after the internship program. They must achieve a cumulative grade point average of 3.0 or higher. Undergraduate applicants must be in their junior year at the time of application. In addition, applicants must submit letters of recommendation and complete a 500-word essay. Undergraduate interns are paid at the GS-6 level, which was approximately $28,085 per year in 2006. Graduate interns are paid at the GS-7 level, which was $31,209 in 2006. Transportation to and from Washington, D.C., is also provided as part of the internship program. For more information on this program, visit https://www.fbijobs.gov/231.asp.

In addition to the Honors Internship Program, the FBI offers several other internship opportunities. Visit https://www.fbijobs.gov/23.asp for more information.

If you are interested in a career with the FBI, you may apply for internships and other programs offered through your local police departments, which will give you experience and insight into aspects of law enforcement in general. Good grades throughout high school and college will give you the best chance of winning a place in the Honors Internship Program.

EMPLOYERS

Agents work for the Federal Bureau of Investigation, which is headquartered in Washington, D.C., and is the investigative arm of the U.S. Department of Justice. Agents are placed in one of 56 field offices or one of 50 foreign liaison posts. The FBI employed 12,659 special agents as of October 31, 2006. The FBI hires on a continual basis, although some years it does not hire any new agents. When the bureau is hiring, it advertises in newspapers, postings, and the Internet.

STARTING OUT

If you are interested in working for the FBI, contact the applicant coordinator at the FBI field office nearest you, or visit the FBI's job Web site, https://www.fbijobs.gov. The bureau will send you information on existing vacancies, requirements for the positions, how to file applications, and locations where examinations will be given. Examinations are scored by computer at FBI headquarters. Interviews are arranged based on the applicant's score and overall qualifications and the agency's current needs.

ADVANCEMENT

FBI promotions are awarded mainly on performance, rather than seniority. All administrative and supervisory jobs are filled from within the ranks by agents who have demonstrated they are able to handle more responsibility. Some FBI agents climb the ladder to become higher-grade administrators and supervisors. For example, an agent may become an inspector, supervisory special agent, or special agent in charge of a field office. Agents may also be assigned to

Learn More About It

Ackerman, Thomas. *FBI Careers: The Ultimate Guide to Landing a Job as One of America's Finest.* 2d ed. Indianapolis, Ind.: Jist Works, 2005.

DeLong, Candice. *Special Agent: My Life On the Front Lines As a Woman in the FBI.* New York: Hyperion, 2001.

Holden, Henry. *To Be an FBI Special Agent.* Osceola, Wisc.: Zenith Press, 2005.

Kessler, Ronald. *The Bureau: The Secret History of the FBI.* New York: St. Martin's Press, 2003.

Kessler, Ronald. *The FBI: Inside the World's Most Powerful Law Enforcement Agency.* New York: Pocket Books, 1994.

Koletar, Joseph W. *The FBI Career Guide: Inside Information on Getting Chosen for And Succeeding in One of the Toughest, Most Prestigious Jobs in the World.* New York: AMACOM, 2006.

Rudman, Jack. *Special Agent FBI.* Syosset, N.Y.: National Learning Corporation, 2004.

Simeone, John. *The Complete Idiot's Guide to the FBI.* Royersford, Penn.: Alpha, 2002.

Theoharis, Athan G. *The FBI: A Comprehensive Reference Guide.* New York: Checkmark Books, 2000.

the FBI headquarters, or they may become headquarters supervisors, unit and section chiefs, and division heads. Agents may retire after 20 years of service, and after the age of 50; mandatory retirement is required at the age of 57. In some instances, agents may be granted one-year extensions up until the age of 60.

EARNINGS

New FBI agents start out at the federal government's GS-10 level— approximately $42,040 in 2006, depending on where the agent lives. Salaries for agents are increased slightly if they reside in cities such as New York, Los Angeles, and Miami that have a high cost of living. Agents also receive an additional 25 percent of their base pay (known as law enforcement availability pay, or LEAP) as compensation for being available 24 hours a day, seven days a week. FBI agents can earn within-grade pay increases upon satisfactory job performance, and grade increases may be earned as the agent gains experience through good job performance. FBI agents in nonsupervisory positions can reach the GS-13 grade—about $65,832 in 2006. Agents who move into management positions can earn a GS-15 salary—about $91,507. Some agents then move into a different employment category called the Senior Executive Service, where they make more than $100,000 annually working for the FBI. Benefits include paid vacation, health and life insurance, retirement, sick leave, and job-related tuition reimbursement.

As federal employees, FBI special agents enjoy generous benefits, including health and life insurance, and 13 days of paid sick leave. Vacation pay begins at 13 days for each of the first three years of service and rises to 20 to 26 days for each year after that. All special agents are required to retire at the age of 57; they may choose to retire at 50 if they have put in 20 years of service.

WORK ENVIRONMENT

Depending on their case assignments, FBI agents may work a very strenuous and variable schedule, frequently working more hours than the customary 40-hour week. They are on call for possible assignment 24 hours a day. Assignments may be given for any location at any time. Every aspect of the agent's work is of a confidential nature. As a result, agents may work under potentially dangerous circumstances in carrying out their assignments, and they may be confronted with unpleasant and even horrifying aspects of life. Because of the confidential nature of their work, they must refrain from speaking about their casework even with relatives or spouses. In addition, agents may be required to travel and perform their duties under many conditions, including severe weather. Nevertheless, a career with the FBI offers a great deal of respect, responsibility, and the possibility of adventure. No two days are ever the same for a special agent.

OUTLOOK

Most job vacancies within the FBI are expected to come as agents retire, advance, or resign. Turnover, in general, has traditionally been low, as most agents remain with the FBI throughout their working lives.

The numbers of FBI special agents are linked to the scope of the FBI's responsibilities. Increases in organized crimes, white-collar crimes, and terrorist threats on American soil have led the FBI to increase the number of agents in recent years.

As the bureau's responsibilities expand, it will create new positions to meet them. Despite increased recruitment, growth in the numbers of new agency hires is expected to remain somewhat limited. Competition for openings will continue to be extremely high. According to the *Chicago Tribune,* the typical recruit is between the ages of 27 and 31, has a graduate level education, and is physically fit. Since the terrorist attacks, the FBI is particularly interested in recruits who are able to speak Arabic and are familiar with Middle and Far Eastern culture. Potential agents with backgrounds in information technology are also in high demand.

FOR MORE INFORMATION

For information on FBI jobs, internship programs (paid and unpaid), current news, and contact information for a field office in your area, visit the FBI Web site. Contact information for your local field office is also available in your telephone directory.

Federal Bureau of Investigation (FBI)
J. Edgar Hoover Building
935 Pennsylvania Avenue, NW
Washington, DC 20535-0001
Tel: 202-324-3000
http://www.fbi.gov

Fire Inspectors and Investigators

OVERVIEW

Fire inspectors perform examinations to enforce fire-prevention laws, ordinances, and codes; promote the development and use of effective fire-prevention methods; and provide instruction to the fire department and the general public regarding fire codes and prevention. They are employed by local fire departments and private companies, including factories, sawmills, chemical plants, and universities. *Fire investigators* analyze the cause, origin, and circumstances of fires involving loss of life and considerable property damage; interrogate witnesses and prepare investigation reports; and arrest and seek prosecution of arsonists. They are employed by local fire departments, state fire marshal's offices, and private companies.

HISTORY

Fire kills more Americans than all natural disasters combined. Each year, approximately 4,000 people die and another 17,000 are injured as a result of fire, according to the National Fire Data Center of the U.S. Fire Administration (USFA). Pinpointing how fires start is an important part of efforts to try to prevent them. Fire inspectors use their knowledge of fire science, building codes, and fire-suppression methods to help eliminate this deadly problem.

Arson is the second leading cause of death in the United States and is the leading cause of property damage due to fires. The USFA estimates that property damage from arson totals more than

QUICK FACTS

School Subjects
Biology
Chemistry

Personal Skills
Leadership/management
Technical/scientific

Work Environment
Indoors and outdoors
Primarily multiple locations

Minimum Education Level
Some postsecondary training

Salary Range
$28,340 to $47,090 to
$100,000+

Certification or Licensing
Recommended

Outlook
Faster than the average

DOT
373

GOE
04.03.01, 04.04.02

NOC
6262

O*NET-SOC
33-2021.00, 33-2021.01,
33-2021.02

$3 billion per year. Determining whether an arsonist caused a fire can help put criminals behind bars, but catching an arsonist is very complicated. According to the USFA, only 15 percent of all arson

A fire inspector dusts a side door of a church for fingerprints after a minor fire. *(Stephan Savoia/AP)*

cases are closed by an arrest. There are three types of fire investigation: fire, arson, and explosion.

THE JOB

Most fire departments are responsible for fire-prevention activities. Fire inspectors inspect buildings and their storage contents for trash, rubbish, and other materials that can ignite easily. They look for worn-out or exposed wiring and for other fire hazards. Inspectors review building and fire-suppression plans to ensure the construction of safe and code-conforming buildings and fire-suppression systems and alarms. They pay close attention to public buildings, such as hospitals, schools, nursing homes, theaters, and hotels, which they inspect regularly. Fire inspectors also ensure that the facility's fire-protection equipment and systems are functioning properly. While inspecting buildings, they might make recommendations on how fire-safety equipment could be used better and provide information regarding the storage of flammable materials, electrical hazards, and other common causes of fires.

Inspectors maintain a variety of reports and records related to fire inspections, code requirements, permits, and training. They also instruct employers, civic groups, schoolchildren, and others on extinguishing small fires, escaping burning buildings, operating fire extinguishers, and establishing evacuation plans.

Fire investigators, or *fire marshals,* look for evidence pointing to the causes of fires. Once fires are extinguished, especially if they are of suspicious origin or cause death or injury, investigators look for evidence of arson, that is, fires that are deliberately set for insurance money or other reasons. Investigators determine whether the fire was incendiary (arson) or accidental, and then try to figure out what caused it and how to prevent it. This information is very important to the fire-protection community, according to Jon C. Jones, a fire-protection consultant in Lumenburg, Massachusetts. He explains that in cases of arson, it is the investigator's responsibility to collect information or evidence that can be used to prosecute the fire starter. For example, the investigator must determine what fuel was used to start the fire and in the process may discover devices that were also used. Investigators may submit reports to a district attorney, testify in court, or arrest suspected arsonists (if investigators have police authority). Investigators also gather information from accidental fires to determine where and how the fire started and how it spread. This is important information because it can be used to prevent similar fires in the future.

Fire investigators also interrogate witnesses, obtain statements and other necessary documentation, and preserve and examine physical and circumstantial evidence. They tour fire scenes and examine debris to collect evidence. Investigators prepare comprehensive reports, provide detailed accounts of investigative procedures, and present findings. They apprehend and arrest arson suspects, as well as seek confinement and control of fire setters and juveniles who set fires. Inspectors also prepare damage estimates for reporting and insurance purposes and compile statistics related to fires and investigations.

REQUIREMENTS

High School

Earning a high school diploma is the first step to becoming a fire inspector or investigator. Take classes in physics, biology, and mathematics. Speech and English courses will help you polish your communication skills.

Postsecondary Training

There are two ways to become a fire inspector. Some fire departments have policies that only those who have served as firefighters can work in the fire-prevention bureau. Other departments want people who are trained primarily for fire prevention. Either way, all students who want to join the fire department, either as an inspector or a firefighter, should take two- or four-year college courses, such as fire service, fire-protection systems, equipment, and fire protection. Specialized fire-prevention classes required for inspectors, such as hazardous materials and processes, flammable liquids, and high-piled stock, can be found through the colleges or the state fire marshal's office. The National Fire Academy (NFA) offers a variety of courses both on and off campus. While the NFA is not an accredited, degree-granting institution, some schools will give college credit for NFA courses. Additionally, NFA has partnered with several colleges across the country that offer bachelor's degrees in the areas of fire administration/management and fire-prevention technology. (Contact information for the NFA is at the end of this article.)

Fire investigators must have knowledge of fire science, chemistry, engineering, and investigative techniques, but a fire-related diploma is not always necessary. An engineering certificate with fire-service experience is sufficient in many cases, depending on the job description and whether the position is in the private (corporate) or public (fire department) sector.

"A law enforcement background is helpful. However, not all investigators will have or need the power of arrest," notes Robert Duval, a fire investigator for the National Fire Protection Association (NFPA) Fire Investigations Department in Quincy, Massachusetts. "Many work in the private sector for insurance companies and other interests. In many municipalities and states, the fire marshal's office handles fire investigations, and most investigators are sworn law enforcement officers."

Certification or Licensing

Most fire departments look for employees who have been educated in fire science. But you do not have to be certified before being hired. Sometimes, an associate's degree is all that is needed. Most people take the majority of their classes while they are working as fire inspectors.

Local regulations may differ, but generally, fire inspectors obtain certification as a fire prevention officer levels 1 and 2 (sometimes 3) from the Office of the State Fire Marshal. Some states also require fire prevention officer levels 1 and 2. There is a series of classes for each level. The International Code Council also offers examination and certification services for fire prevention inspector 1 and 2. The Uniform Fire Code, as well as the Uniform Building Code, provides code requirements on building construction, fire-prevention regulations, and system maintenance.

The main certification process for fire investigators is certified fire investigator, which is administered by the International Association of Arson Investigators. There is no straight path to becoming a fire investigator, and it is not an entry-level job. Most of the investigators who come from fire departments start out in the fire-prevention bureau. Others come from police departments. Fire investigation is a multidisciplinary field, which requires skills in many areas, including fire fighting, law enforcement, mechanical engineering, mathematics, and chemical engineering.

Other Requirements

"Good fire inspectors enjoy working with people," says Rochelle Maurer, a fire-prevention officer for the Torrance Fire Department in Torrance, California. "They need to be flexible and sensitive to the business owners' needs, but they also need to strictly enforce the fire and building codes when public safety is involved. In a sense, inspectors are salespeople. In many cases, business owners will be spending money to be in compliance with the fire and building codes. Inspectors must have the ability to sell the idea of fire prevention and compliance."

Robert Duval adds: "[Fire] investigators should be well-organized in the field as well as in the office. If you are not well-organized in the field, you might not get the information you seek, and if your notes and diagrams are a mess, then the report-writing portion of the job will take longer."

Investigators should be in good physical condition to adapt to extreme weather or fire-scene conditions and should be able to withstand long hours in unfavorable conditions. Most of all, Duval points out, investigators must have a great deal of integrity. Without this, they will not be credible witnesses in court.

EXPLORING

Although you can't begin investigating fires on your own, you can, nevertheless, become familiar with the fire safety and science field through a number of activities. First, visit the Fire Safety for Citizens section of the U.S. Fire Administration's Web site, http://www.usfa. dhs.gov/citizens. This source has fire-safety tips, publications, facts about fires, and more. You can also visit the U.S. Fire Administration's main Web page (http://www.usfa.fema.gov) to find information on topics such as the National Fire Academy, data and statistics, and research.

Once you have done some reading on the field, you may want to contact a professional for more information. Your school guidance counselor or a teacher can help arrange for a visit to a local fire department for a tour of the facilities, where you may also have the opportunity to talk with firefighters about their work. An informational interview with a fire inspector or investigator can also provide you with insights.

Many fire departments have volunteer programs. Find out if there are any in your area and sign up to volunteer if you meet their requirements. Keep in good physical shape because this is important for any fire-safety professional. You can also add to your skills by taking CPR and first-aid classes.

EMPLOYERS

Local fire departments, individual state fire marshal offices, insurance companies, and private industry employ fire inspectors and investigators. Others work independently as consultants.

STARTING OUT

Those just starting out in this field will need to determine if they need to gain experience as a professional firefighter before moving into the position of fire inspector. (As mentioned previously, this varies by department.) To become a firefighter, you must pass the local civil service exam, pass physical training, and complete training at the department's training center or academy. Those who have earned degrees, for example, in fire protection engineering, may find information on job openings through their schools' placement centers. Jobs can also be found through organizations, such as the NFPA.

ADVANCEMENT

Fire inspectors can be promoted to officers or heads of fire-prevention bureaus, fire marshals, or chief building officials. Fire-inspection workers in factories can become plant fire marshals and corporate or plant risk managers. Fire investigators can rise in rank within the department. Many become lieutenants, captains, and fire marshals within their jurisdictions.

EARNINGS

Inspector salaries depend primarily on two things: if they work in the public or private sector and how large those departments or companies are. Typical salaries range from $30,000 to $45,000 to $75,000 and can increase with experience and years with the organization.

Fire inspectors and investigators earned a median annual salary of $47,090 in 2005, according to the U.S. Department of Labor. Ten percent earned less than $28,340, and the highest 10 percent of all inspectors and investigators earned more than $73,770. Fire inspectors and investigators in local government jobs earned approximately $49,830 a year. As in all occupations, the experts demand higher salaries, so private sector investigators' salaries can go much higher (to the $100,000+ range) if they work as national expert witnesses.

WORK ENVIRONMENT

Fire inspectors usually spend a few hours in the morning in their offices or at the fire department. From there, they spend most of the day out in the field. There is no set timetable for investigators. They may spend days at a time in the field conducting scene surveys and

A Typical Day on the Job

Fire Prevention Officer Rochelle Maurer of the Torrance Fire Department in Torrance, California, describes a typical day:

"You don't have to be a jock to be an inspector. I have one-half of a kneecap that prevents me from being a firefighter, but I have the education and 18 years of experience I need to be an inspector, which helps me still be a part of the fire service.

"Each morning, the fire marshal and inspectors meet. Each inspector is assigned a specific area of town. The majority of inspections are surprises for business owners and can include such places as restaurants and new construction for sprinklers and fire alarm systems. Next stop could be a complaint of weeds or possible fire hazards in someone's backyard. You might act as a fire safety officer during the making of movies and commercials. Then, you could meet with a contractor or architect to discuss fire and life safety issues for a new building. Inspectors are always needed to provide technical assistance to an engine company of firefighters who are performing company inspections. The day always ends with paperwork and returning phone calls.

"The hardest part of the job is the amount of paperwork. Good writing skills are very important. Inspectors document all types of businesses, the chemicals they use, and any code violations. These files inform the businesses of what they need to correct to be in compliance and note information that is crucial for fire department operations, including possible hazards for responding emergency personnel.

"Each day offers a variety of fun and challenging issues. Inspectors are not tied to their desks. Your daily activities can take you from a manufacturing plant to a hospital to a movie shoot. Statistics show that with the increase in fire prevention activities, fires and fire deaths have been reduced. It is a great feeling knowing you are a part of it."

interviewing involved parties and then spend the next several days or weeks in the office preparing the reports.

OUTLOOK

The outlook for fire inspectors is about the same as for firefighters. Employment should grow faster than the average for all occupations through 2014, according to the U.S. Department of Labor. Fire investigators have an even better employment outlook than fire inspectors, since there will always be fires to investigate. This field is constantly being advanced by new technology and remains one of the most interesting aspects of the fire service.

FOR MORE INFORMATION

For information on the investigation of arson, contact
International Association of Arson Investigators
2151 Priest Bridge Drive, Suite 25
Crofton, MD 2114-2427
Tel: 410-451-3473
http://www.firearson.com

For certification information, contact
International Code Council
500 New Jersey Avenue, NW, 6th Floor
Washington, DC 20001-2070
Tel: 888-422-7233
http://www.iccsafe.org

The National Fire Academy provides training both at its campus and through distance education. Through the Degrees at a Distance Program, the National Fire Academy works with several colleges across the country to offer bachelor's degrees in fire administration/management and fire prevention technology.
National Fire Academy
16825 South Seton Avenue
Emmitsburg, MD 21727-8920
Tel: 301-447-1000
http://www.usfa.fema.gov/fire-service/nfa/nfa.shtm

For information on fire prevention careers, certification, and news, contact
National Fire Protection Association
One Batterymarch Park
Quincy, MA 02169-7471
Tel: 617-770-3000
Email: public_affairs@nfpa.org
http://www.nfpa.org

Fire Safety Technicians

QUICK FACTS

School Subjects
Chemistry
Mathematics

Personal Skills
Following instructions
Technical/scientific

Work Environment
Indoors and outdoors
One location with some
  travel

Minimum Education Level
Associate's degree

Salary Range
$20,500 to $38,500 to
  $100,000+

Certification or Licensing
Recommended

Outlook
Faster than the average

DOT
373

GOE
04.04.01

NOC
6262

O*NET-SOC
17-2111.02

OVERVIEW

Fire safety technicians work to prevent fires. Typical services they perform include conducting safety inspections and planning fire protection systems. In the course of their job, fire safety technicians recognize fire hazards, apply technical knowledge, and perform services to control and prevent fires. There are approximately 353,000 fire department workers. However, only a small percentage of these are technically prepared inspectors, supervisors, or technical workers.

HISTORY

Fires in homes and at workplaces are the greatest destroyers of human life and property. Every year thousands of people in the United States die due to fires. Property destroyed by fire costs billions of dollars each year. In some states, grass or brush fires periodically rage uncontrolled and advance at the speed of the wind; buildings are destroyed and livestock is lost. Forest fires consume millions of feet of lumber every year. Some fires increase the problems of wildlife conservation and flood control, requiring that considerable sums be spent on reforestation programs.

In the early days of the United States, fire protection was usually left to a few volunteers in a community. This group formed a fire brigade and had simple firefighting devices. Later, fire departments were established and firefighting equipment became more sophisticated. Even so, fire protection was still mostly left to a small group. As cities grew and large industrial plants were built, it became apparent that fire prevention was possibly even more important than firefighting skills and techniques.

Today, business and industrial firms realize that fire protection is one of the most important considerations in the construction and operation of their plants. Fire insurance rates are determined by fire probability factors, such as the type of construction, ease of transporting personnel, and the quality and quantity of fire protection equipment available. Managers realize that payments from fire insurance claims will not cover the total loss caused by fire—lost production or sales. Employees expect their employers to have warning systems and fire-extinguishing devices. The public expects fire departments to be well staffed with competent specialists and firefighters who can minimize property damage and save lives. Their jobs involve rescuing people from fire, giving safety education courses, and conducting inspections, which may include a thorough examination of exits, corridors, and stairways designed to carry traffic in an emergency.

The need for carefully planned, well-organized fire protection has created a demand for highly trained personnel. Specialists are needed who are skilled in the newest methods of fire prevention and fire fighting. Such specialists are also familiar with new synthetic materials used in building construction, decorative drapes, floor coverings, furnishings, and even clothing. These materials have made fire protection more complicated because of the toxic fumes they produce when burned.

Because of all of these factors, an increasing number of well-trained fire safety technicians are being hired by business, industry, and other employers to prevent loss of life and property from fires while people are on the job, in school, in recreational or entertainment places, or traveling.

THE JOB

Fire safety technicians are employed by local fire departments, fire insurance companies, industrial organizations, government agencies, and businesses dealing with fire-protection equipment and consulting services.

Fire science specialists employed by insurance companies make recommendations for fire protection and safety measures in specific buildings. As part of their duties, they help set insurance rates, examine water supply and sprinkler facilities, and make suggestions to correct hazardous conditions. They may be part of an arson investigation squad or work with adjusters to determine the amount of personal injury or property loss caused by fire.

In industry, fire safety technicians are often part of an industrial safety team. They inspect areas for possible fire hazards and formulate company procedures in case of fire. They make periodic inspections of firefighting equipment such as extinguishers, hoses and hydrants, fire doors, automatic alarms, and sprinkler systems. An important part of their duties is to hold fire-prevention seminars to keep department heads and key workers aware and alert to potential fire hazards in their particular areas. Technicians also teach these employees what to do in case of fire or other emergencies.

Because of the large number of people occupying their facilities, many restaurants, large hotels, and entertainment or recreational centers employ fire safety technicians. There is a great hazard of fire from food cooking in kitchens, lint in laundries, and sparks that fall on draperies and bedding. The possible loss of life from fire makes it necessary to have the best possible fire-protection program.

Many government agencies employ fire safety technicians. They are largely responsible for inspecting government buildings, property and storage, or handling systems for reducing fire hazards. They arrange for installation of adequate alarm systems and fire-protection devices. They may be required to organize a firefighting unit in a government agency or assist with designing sprinkler systems in buildings.

Companies that manufacture fire-protection devices and alarm systems employ many technicians. Their training enables them to explain technical functions to customers and to give advice on installation and use. They also help to place smoke detectors and other fire-prevention or extinguishing devices in the correct locations to give the greatest protection from fire, and they service fire-protection devices after they are installed. Fire extinguishers, for example, must be regularly inspected to be certain that they function properly. *Fire extinguisher servicers* are technicians trained to perform inspections, tests, and maintenance of fire extinguishers and may also instruct people on their use. Private companies specializing in fire-safety equipment often employ them.

Public education is also an important area of activity for fire control and safety technicians. By working with the public through schools, businesses, and service clubs and organizations, they can expand the level of understanding about the dangers of fire and teach people about methods of fire protection and fire prevention.

Newly hired technicians generally receive on-the-job orientation before they are given full responsibility in an entry-level position. Examples of entry-level positions are described in the following paragraphs:

Fire insurance inspectors inspect buildings and offices and make recommendations for fire protection and general safety conditions.

Fire insurance underwriters help set rates to conform to company policies and building codes.

Fire insurance adjusters determine losses due to fire and compute rates for adjustment and settling claims.

Fire protection engineering technicians draft plans for the installation of fire protection systems for buildings and structures. Using their knowledge of drafting and fire-protection codes, they analyze architectural blueprints and specifications to determine which type and size of fire-protection system is required to meet fire-protection codes and then estimate its cost. During building construction, they work with the superintendent to ensure proper installation of the system. They may specialize in a specific kind of fire-protection system, such as foam, water, dry chemicals, or gas. After a fire, they may inspect fire-damaged buildings to check for malfunctioning systems.

Fire inspectors check firefighting equipment and report any potential fire hazards. They recommend changes in equipment, practice, materials, or methods to reduce fire hazards. (For more information on this career, see the article Fire Inspectors and Investigators.)

Plant protection inspectors inspect industrial plants for fire hazards, report findings, and recommend action.

Fire alarm superintendents inspect alarm systems in government buildings and institutions.

Fire service field instructors hold training sessions throughout a state to keep firefighters up-to-date on firefighting methods and techniques. They may also inspect small fire departments and report on personnel and equipment.

REQUIREMENTS

While a high school diploma is often sufficient to obtain employment as a firefighter, aspiring fire safety technicians should plan to attend a two-year, postsecondary program in fire technology or a four-year program in fire-protection engineering.

High School

While in high school, you should study the physical sciences. You should take either physics or chemistry courses that include laboratory work. Fire science demands some knowledge of hydraulics, physics, and chemistry. For example, laying out sprinkler systems requires skills that are introduced in high school mechanical drawing courses. Algebra and geometry are also recommended, as well as English and writing courses.

Postsecondary Training

Two-year, postsecondary fire-technology programs are now available at more than 100 technical institutes and community colleges. These programs provide in-depth education in the fire-science specialization for people seeking to work for industries, institutions, or government as fire safety technicians. These programs are also available to members of fire departments or related fire specialists.

Courses in these programs include physics and hydraulics, as they apply to pump and nozzle pressures. Fundamentals of chemistry are taught to help students understand chemical methods of extinguishing fires and the chemistry of materials and combustion. Communications skills are also emphasized.

Typical courses in the first year of a two-year program include firefighting tactics and strategy, fire-protection equipment and alarm systems, fundamentals of fire suppression, introductory fire technology, chemistry (especially combustion and chemistry of materials), mathematics, and communications skills.

Second-year courses may include building construction for fire protection, hazardous materials, fire administration, industrial-fire protection, applied physics, introduction to fire prevention, and applied economics.

Like most professional workers in high-technology careers, fire safety technicians must continue to study during their careers to keep up with new developments in their field. Improved fire detection and prevention instruments, equipment, and methods for making materials fireproof are being developed all the time.

Certification or Licensing

The Board of Certified Safety Professionals (BCSP) offers the designations associate safety professional (ASP) and certified safety professional (CSP). Although the BCSP does not offer a specific certification unique to fire safety technicians, anyone wishing to advance in the field of fire safety should get the ASP and CSP designations. These credentials demonstrate that the technician has completed a high level of education, has passed written examinations, and has acquired a certain amount of professional experience.

The National Institute for Certification in Engineering Technologies offers certification to fire-protection workers in the following specialty areas: Automatic Sprinkler System Layout, Fire Alarm Systems, Inspection and Testing of Water-Based Systems, and Special Hazards Suppression Systems. Contact the institute for information on requirements for each certification.

Other Requirements

Those who wish to work in fire-science technology in fire departments may train as technicians and apply for specialist jobs in large fire departments. Others may choose to enter the fire department as untrained firefighters. For the latter group, very rigid physical examinations are usually required. Firefighters must keep themselves physically fit and conditioned since they may be required to do hard work in all types of weather and sometimes for long hours.

Firefighters must be able to follow orders and to accept the discipline that is necessary for effective teamwork. While on active call, firefighters usually work under the close supervision of commanding officers such as battalion chiefs or assistant fire chiefs. Their work requires highly organized team efforts to be effective, since there is usually a great deal of excitement and confusion at fires.

Because of the physical demands of the profession, physical-performance tests are required and may include running, climbing, and jumping. These examinations are clearly defined by local civil service regulations but may vary from one community to another.

In most cases, prospective firefighters must be at least 18 years of age. They must also meet height and weight requirements. Applicants must have good vision (20/20 vision is required in some departments), no hindering physical impairments, and strong stamina. Some fire departments require that applicants be nonsmokers.

"The most important requirements are dedication and the ability to communicate well," says Assistant Chief Daniel J. Voiland of the Naperville Fire Department, Naperville, Illinois.

Fire science technicians, who do not work as firefighters but as industrial or government inspectors and consultants, do not need unusual physical strength. These technicians must be able to read and write with ease and communicate well in order to study technical information and give good written or oral reports.

For fire safety technicians in industry or government, no licenses are usually required. Favorable academic records and an appropriate two-year degree or certificate are given special consideration by most employers. Becoming a member of the Society of Fire Protection Engineers is a valuable mark of achievement of which employers take note.

For those who want to enter fire departments as firefighters and work toward technician-level tasks, civil service examinations are required in most cases.

Firefighters are a highly organized occupational group; many firefighters belong to the International Association of Fire Fighters.

EXPLORING

If your are still in high school, your guidance department and science teachers should be able to provide you with some introductory information about the various careers in fire protection, safety, and prevention. You can visit your local fire department, look at the equipment, and talk with the firefighters and their commanding officers. In some departments, you may be able to gain experience by working as a volunteer firefighter.

"Many departments have Fire Explorer Posts," notes Daniel Voiland. "Local or community colleges also have courses in fire science and prevention that high school students can take."

Courses in lifesaving and first aid also offer helpful experience. Summer jobs as aides with the government park and forest service are available as well. In these jobs, you may learn about fire prevention, control, and detection in forest and grassland conservation work.

It is usually possible to arrange a visit with an insurance company to learn about the huge economic losses caused by fire. Large insurance offices often have agents or officers who can describe fire technician jobs or services in inspection, fire insurance, rate setting or claim settlement, and fire-prevention services. You can also obtain part-time or summer jobs with fire-equipment manufacturing, supply, and service companies.

EMPLOYERS

Challenging job opportunities are available for fire safety technicians. Most are employed by public or private fire departments and the rest work for large corporations overseeing the design and operation of fire-prevention systems. Insurance companies hire fire safety technicians to survey the facilities they insure and to perform research, testing, and analysis. Fire safety technicians and fire protection engineers work in various levels of government and in branches of the armed services, where they help develop and enforce building and fire-prevention codes. Fire safety technicians also work for fire equipment and systems manufacturing companies, hospitals and health care facilities, industrial and chemical companies, testing and certifying laboratories, transportation companies, and universities and colleges.

STARTING OUT

Graduates of two-year programs in technical colleges, community colleges, or technical institutes usually secure jobs before they graduate. They are hired by company recruiters sent to school career services offices, which arrange interviews for graduating students. The placement officers or fire science instructors usually keep contacts open to help place their current graduates.

Some schools have cooperative work-study programs where students study part time and work part time for pay. Employers who participate in cooperative programs provide experience in different tasks so the student learns about various aspects of the job. Often, the cooperating employer hires students in such programs for permanent jobs.

Some students may find jobs in fire departments that are large enough to need special technicians outside the ranks of regular firefighters. Others may choose to become firefighters and advance to technical positions.

Some fire departments place new employees on probation, a period during which they are intensively trained. After training is completed, they may be assigned to specific duties.

Students with a high school diploma or its equivalent can enter a fire department apprenticeship program. These programs run from three to four years, combining intensive on-the-job training with active firefighting service, and include related study in the science and theory of firefighting. These apprenticeship programs may or may not be union-sponsored.

Even after completing an apprenticeship program, fire safety technicians seeking to advance to the level of supervisor or inspector must continue to study. Part-time courses are available in community colleges or technical institutes.

In some small communities, applicants may enter through on-the-job training as volunteer firefighters or by direct application for such an appointment.

ADVANCEMENT

Examples of advanced positions are described in the following paragraphs:

Fire prevention analysts analyze overall fire-prevention systems in an organization and confer with fire inspectors to obtain detailed information and recommend policies and programs for fire prevention.

Fire protection engineers combine their engineering and management skills to perform a broad range of jobs. Some work as *fire protection designers,* creating systems that automatically detect and suppress fires. Some design fire alarm, smoke control, emergency lighting, communication, and exit systems. These engineers also perform fire-safety evaluations of buildings and industrial complexes. Some research the behavior and control of fire. Others analyze risk management and assessment for industrial applications. Fire protection engineers also investigate fires or explosions, preparing technical reports or providing expert courtroom testimony on the facts of the incident.

"The difference between fire safety technicians and fire protection engineers is that the engineers usually look at the big picture," according to Morgan Hurley, technical director at the Society of Fire Protection Engineers. "Technicians specialize in one specific system, such as sprinklers or smoke alarms. Engineers expand on that knowledge."

Deputy fire marshals inspect possible fire hazards and analyze the amount of loss resulting from a fire. If necessary, they have the authority to condemn buildings. They report cases of arson and work with district attorneys to prosecute arsonists. This is an appointed position, although those holding the position usually have considerable fire experience.

Fire captains work under the supervision of a *fire chief* on a military base or in a municipal area. They are responsible for fire protection in a specific location. Fire chiefs are responsible for all firefighting units in a municipal area. Several fire captains may report to and support the activities of this administrator.

"Other advancements include an officer position in the fire-prevention bureau or branching out into the building department," says Daniel Voiland.

Owners of fire equipment or consulting businesses employ *fire prevention and control technicians and specialists*, who contract for, deliver, and install equipment and provide training and other services in fire prevention.

EARNINGS

Beginning salaries for fire safety technicians tend to be higher than those of other technicians. This is partly due to the shortage of qualified personnel in the field. Starting salaries are approximately $20,500 to $22,000. Experienced technicians earn salaries that average between $33,000 to $44,000 per year. Those who advance to positions of great responsibility may earn $60,000 per year or more.

The Society of Fire Protection Engineers reports that the average starting salary for fire protection engineers was $47,000 in 2005. Professionals with considerable experience had mean earnings of $85,000. Top engineers can earn more than $100,000 annually. According to the International City-County Management Association, fire prevention/code inspectors earned salaries that ranged from $43,297 to $54,712 in 2004.

Benefits usually include compensatory time off or overtime pay for hours worked beyond the regular work schedule. Other benefits include liberal pension plans, disability benefits, and early retirement options. Also included are paid vacations, paid sick leave, and in some cases, paid holidays or compensatory time off for holidays worked.

WORK ENVIRONMENT

Fire safety technicians may experience danger when assisting or observing firefighting or when inspecting and analyzing structures damaged or destroyed by fire. Floors, walls, or entire buildings can collapse on firefighters as they work to save lives and property. Exposure to smoke, fumes, chemicals, and gases can injure or kill. Most of the duties, however, are performed in offices where the surroundings are clean, safe, and comfortable.

When performing routine inspections, these workers must follow safety regulations and wear protective clothing when appropriate. They must be familiar with the environments they inspect and analyze.

Fire safety technicians must have a natural curiosity about everything that relates to fire. They must be patient and willing to study the physics and chemistry of fire, as well as fire prevention and control. They must also be able to think systematically and objectively as they analyze fire hazards, damages, and prevention.

Technicians must be observant and understand how human factors of carelessness, thoughtlessness, fatigue, or haste may cause fires. One of the great challenges of this career is to learn how to teach people to avoid the mistakes that cause fires and to establish safety procedures and controls that prevent fires.

Fire is one of the most feared and destructive hazards. Fire science technicians can find continuing satisfaction and challenge in saving lives and property by preventing fires. "The hardest part is finding out why systems did not pass inspection," Daniel Voiland notes, "but the best part is ensuring the buildings in the community are safe."

OUTLOOK

Technical careers in fire prevention and control are predicted to grow more rapidly than the average for all other occupations. In the future, these technicians will probably be needed in more places than ever before. The greatest increase in employment will be in industry. More industries are finding that the cost of replacing buildings and property destroyed by fire is greater than the yearly cost of fire protection and the expertise and equipment of these specialists.

New fire prevention and control techniques must be developed as technology continues to change. Skilled and ambitious fire safety technicians will be needed to address and monitor this changing technology.

FOR MORE INFORMATION

The following organization offers general information on careers in fire safety
American Society of Safety Engineers
1800 East Oakton Street
Des Plaines, IL 60018-2187
Tel: 847-699-2929
Email: customerservice@asse.org
http://www.asse.org

For information on the ASP and CSP certifications, contact
Board of Certified Safety Professionals
208 Burwash Avenue
Savoy, IL 61874-9510
Tel: 217-359-9263
http://www.bcsp.com

For information on fire prevention careers, contact
National Fire Protection Association
One Batterymarch Park
Quincy, MA 02169-7471
Tel: 617-770-3000
Email: public_affairs@nfpa.org
http://www.nfpa.org

For information on training programs, contact
National Fire Sprinkler Association
40 Jon Barrett Road
Patterson, NY 12563-1000
Tel: 845-878-4200, ext. 133

Email: info@nfsa.org
http://www.nfsa.org

For information on certification, contact
National Institute for Certification in Engineering Technologies
1420 King Street
Alexandria, VA 22314-2794
Tel: 888-476-4238
http://www.nicet.org

For information on student chapters, a list of universities that offer programs in fire protection engineering, and a copy of Careers in Fire Protection Engineering, *contact*
Society of Fire Protection Engineers
7315 Wisconsin Avenue, Suite 620E
Bethesda, MD 20814-3234
Tel: 301-718-2910
http://www.sfpe.org

Firefighters

QUICK FACTS

School Subjects
Biology
Chemistry

Personal Skills
Leadership/management
Mechanical/manipulative

Work Environment
Indoors and outdoors
Primarily multiple locations

Minimum Education Level
High school diploma

Salary Range
$19,730 to $39,090 to
$92,780+

Certification or Licensing
Recommended

Outlook
Faster than the average

DOT
373

GOE
04.04.01

NOC
6262

O*NET-SOC
33-2011.00

OVERVIEW

Firefighters are responsible for protecting people's lives and property from the hazards of fire and other emergencies. They provide this protection by fighting fires to prevent property damage and by rescuing people trapped or injured by fires or other accidents. Through inspections and safety education, firefighters also work to prevent fires and unsafe conditions that could result in dangerous, life-threatening situations. They assist in many types of emergencies and disasters in everyday life. Although in many rural areas firefighters serve on a volunteer basis, this article is mainly concerned with describing full-time career firefighters. There are approximately 282,000 paid firefighters working in the United States.

HISTORY

Civilization would not exist without fire, but this essential tool can often become destructive and deadly. For centuries, people have fought to protect their lives and property from fire. In biblical times, people would group themselves into brigades to form firefighting lines. American colonists used the bucket brigade to pass water from person to person in combating fires. Benjamin Franklin in Philadelphia formed the first permanent firefighting company in 1736. New York established its own fire company in 1737, and the practice spread through the other colonies. At the same time, volunteer fire brigades supplemented these professional firefighters.

The growth of U.S. cities during the 19th century led to an increased need for professional firefighters and better equipment.

Many cities suffered devastating fires. Crowded conditions, poor building techniques and materials, the lack of a sufficient water supply, and the absence of coordinated, citywide fire services meant that even a small fire could have terrible consequences. In 1871, for example, fire swept through Chicago, destroying virtually the entire city. The poor equipment available to them also hampered firefighters. Many museums house some of the old firefighting equipment that was invented during this time, such as hand-pulled vehicles with water tanks that were pumped to direct a stream of water through a hose onto a fire. In those days, the tanks were still filled by bucket brigades. This equipment was an improvement, but still grossly inadequate for fighting larger fires. Many of these vehicles were themselves destroyed by fire; since the hand-pumped force of the water was weak, and the hoses were short and stiff, the vehicles had to be positioned close to the fires. Another difficulty in fighting fires was that many firefighters, especially the volunteers, were poorly trained, if at all.

As automobiles, trucks, and industrial machinery were invented and improved, new and better firefighting equipment was also created. By the turn of the century, almost every large city in the United States had organized professional, paid fire departments, with steam-powered fire engines and a system of fire hydrants to provide an adequate supply of water wherever a fire occurred. The development of the telegraph enabled cities to establish telegraph alarm systems, allowing fire departments to respond more quickly in the early stages of a fire. Other scientific advancements have also made contributions, such as the invention of the fire extinguisher. Firefighters began to receive training in many firefighting techniques. A system of building codes was established, which governed the construction of buildings to prevent fires and to prevent a fire in one building from spreading to other buildings nearby. Eventually, these codes included requirements for smoke alarms, sprinkler systems, fire drills, and other measures to reduce the incidence of fires and the loss of life associated with them.

Today, there are more than 30,000 organized fire departments across the United States, with approximately 282,000 professional, salaried firefighters. Nevertheless, thousands of people are injured or killed each year due to fire. The National Fire Data Center reports that fires caused injuries to 17,925 Americans and 3,675 deaths in 2005. In addition, 115 firefighters were killed while on duty. In 2001, firefighter deaths were especially high (at an estimated 441), with 343 firefighters dying during rescue efforts at the World Trade Center in New York City on September 11. This occurrence, the worst single-incident loss of firefighter lives in history, clearly illustrates firefighters' commitment to service as they risk their own lives to protect the lives of others.

THE JOB

The duties of career firefighters vary with the size of the fire department and the population of the city in which they are employed. However, each firefighter's individual responsibilities are well defined and clear-cut. In every fire department there are divisions of labor among firefighters. For example, when their department goes into action, firefighters know whether they are to rescue people caught in fires, raise ladders, connect hoses to water hydrants, or attempt to break down doors, windows, or walls with fire axes so that other firefighters can enter the area with water hoses.

Firefighters may fight a fire in a massive building giving off intense heat, or they may be called to extinguish nothing more than a small brush fire or a blazing garbage can. Firefighters on duty at fire stations must be prepared to go on an alarm call at any moment. Time wasted may result in more damage or even loss of life. Firefighters wear protective suits to prevent their hands and bodies from injury, including protective gloves, helmets, boots, coats, and self-contained breathing apparatuses. Because of the mass confusion that occurs at the scene of a fire and the dangerous nature of the work, the firefighters are organized into details and units. They work under the supervision of commanding officers, such as fire captains, battalion chiefs, or the fire chief. These officers may reassign the firefighters' duties at any time, depending on the needs of a particular situation.

Once firefighters have extinguished a fire, they often remain at the site for a certain length of time to make sure that the fire is completely out. *Fire investigators* or *fire marshals* may examine the scene to determine the causes of the fire, especially if it resulted in injury or death or may have been set intentionally. They seek clues to the type of fuel or the place where the fire may have started. They may also determine that the fire was the result of arson—that is, it was set deliberately—and they will examine the scene for evidence that will lead them to suspects. These officials may arrest suspected arsonists and testify in court against them.

Firefighters often answer calls requesting emergency medical care, such as help in giving artificial respiration to drowning victims or emergency aid for heart attack victims on public streets. They may also administer emergency medical care. Many fire departments

Firefighters work together to control a fire in a nearby building.
(Photodisc)

operate emergency medical services. Most firefighters are cross-trained to participate in both fire and emergency activities.

Some firefighters are assigned as *fire inspectors*. Their work is to prevent fires. They inspect buildings for trash, chemicals, and other materials that could easily ignite; for poor, worn-out, or exposed wiring; for inadequate alarm systems, blocked hallways, or impassable exits; and for other conditions that pose fire hazards. These conditions are usually reported to the owners of the property for correction; if not corrected, the owners could be fined and held criminally liable if any fires occur. Fire inspectors also check to see that public buildings are operated in accordance with fire codes and city ordinances and that the building management complies with safety regulations and fire precautions. Often firefighters are called on to give speeches on fire prevention before school and civic groups.

While firefighters are on station duty and between alarm calls, they perform various duties on a regular basis. They must keep all firefighting equipment in first-class condition for immediate use. This includes polishing and lubricating mechanical equipment, keeping water hoses dry and stretched into shape, and keeping their own personal protective gear in good repair. They hold practice drills for improving response times and firefighting techniques to become as efficient and proficient as possible.

Many firefighters study while on duty to improve their skills and knowledge of fire fighting and emergency medical techniques. They also prepare themselves for examinations, which are given regularly and which determine to some extent their opportunities for promotion. They are often required to participate in training programs to hone their skills and learn new techniques.

Since many firefighters must live at the fire station for periods of 24 hours at a time, housekeeping duties and cleaning chores are performed by the on-duty firefighters on a rotation basis. In some small towns, firefighters are only employed on a part-time basis. They are on alarm call from their homes, except perhaps for practice drills. Usually in such situations, only a fire chief and assistant live at the station and are employed full time.

Firefighters work in other settings as well. Many industrial plants employ fire marshals who are in charge of fire-prevention and firefighting efforts and personnel. At airports, potential or actual airplane crashes bring out crash, fire, and rescue workers who prevent or put out fires and save passengers and crewmembers.

The job of firefighters has become more complicated in recent years due to the use of increasingly sophisticated equipment. In addition, many firefighters have assumed additional responsibilities. For example, firefighters work with emergency medical services providing emergency medical treatment, assisting in the rescue and recovery from natural disasters such as earthquakes and tornadoes, as well as manmade disasters, such as the control and cleanup of oil spills and other hazardous chemical incidents, or rescuing victims of bombings. The work of firefighters is very dangerous. The nature of the work demands training, practice, courage, and teamwork. However, firefighting is more than a physical activity that requires strength and alertness. It is also a science that demands continual study and learning.

REQUIREMENTS

High School

Most job opportunities open to firefighters today require applicants to have a high school education. "Today's firefighter needs to have a good understanding of the sciences, as much of what line firefighters do revolves around emergency medical services and the extinguishment of fire," says Chief Randy Bruegman, Clackamas County Fire District, Milwaukie, Oregon. "Therefore, classes in related sciences such as anatomy, physics, and biology are very helpful."

Postsecondary Training
Once high school is completed, there are a variety of options available in both two- and four-year degree programs that specifically focus on fire science and emergency medical certificates. Both are extremely helpful when competing for a position.

In most cases, applicants are required to pass written intelligence tests. Some municipalities may require a civil service examination. Formal education is an asset to potential firefighters because part of their training involves a continuous education program, and a person's educational progress may affect future opportunities for advancement.

Many junior and community colleges offer two-year fire-technology programs. Courses involve the study of physics and hydraulics as they apply to pump and nozzle pressures. Fundamentals of chemistry are taught to provide an understanding of chemical methods of extinguishing fires. Skill in communications—both written and spoken—is also emphasized.

Beginning firefighters may receive six to 12 or more weeks of intensive training, either as on-the-job training or through formal fire department training schools. Training is given both in the classroom and in the field, where new firefighters are taught the fundamentals of firefighting, fire prevention, ventilation, emergency medical procedures, the use and care of equipment, and general job duties and skills, including search and rescue techniques. Trainees may also be given instruction in local building codes and fire ordinances. After this period, new firefighters generally serve a six-month to one-year probationary apprenticeship. Apprentice firefighters usually start out on the job as ladder handlers or hose handlers and are given additional responsibilities with training and experience.

Certification or Licensing
Regulations vary by state, but firefighters do not generally need certification before they are hired, and certification is voluntary but recommended. Certification is typically offered through a state's fire academy, fire-service certification board, fire-service training board, or other agency regulating fire and public safety personnel. Certification programs are accredited by the International Fire Service Accreditation Congress (IFSAC), which provides a listing of states offering the Firefighter I and Firefighter II designations.

To become certified, candidates must pass written and practical tests. (Contact information for the IFSAC is at the end of this article.)

Other Requirements

Very strict physical examinations are usually required for the job of firefighter. Applicants must also pass rigorous physical performance tests, which may include running, climbing, and jumping. These examinations are clearly defined by local civil service regulations.

In most cases, firefighters must be at least 18 years of age. Generally, the age range for becoming a professional firefighter is between 18 and 35. Candidates must also meet height and weight requirements. Applicants are required to have good vision (20/20 vision is required in some departments), no physical impairments that could keep them from doing their jobs, and great physical stamina. Many cities have residency requirements for their fire department personnel. Most firefighters join the International Association of Fire Fighters (AFL-CIO) when they are hired.

Usually, the individuals who score the highest on their tests have the best chances of getting jobs as firefighters. Those who gained firefighting experience in the military or who have served as volunteer community firefighters may receive preferential consideration on their job applications. Applicants with emergency medical service and training are often in demand as firefighters.

A mechanical aptitude is an asset to a person in this career. Also important are a congenial temperament and the ability to adapt to uncertain situations that call for teamwork. Firefighters must be willing to follow the orders of their superiors. Firefighters need sound judgment, mental alertness, and the ability to reason and think logically in situations demanding courage and bravery. The ability to remain calm and compassionate is a valued asset, as firefighters must cope with the emotions of those they are helping, emotions that range from those of distraught homeowners to burn victims.

"Firefighters must have the willingness to provide service over one's self," says Chief Bruegman. "The qualities that we look for include someone who is willing to work hard, has a commitment to serve others, and is a team player. The shifts that firefighters work are 24 hours on and 48 hours off, and, with a variety of schedules in between, it is crucial that they have personalities that can interact well in that type of environment. We also look for people who can speak well in public, articulate and teach, and can react well in a variety of situations, whether it is in a public education forum or on an emergency scene."

EXPLORING

You can explore this occupation by talking with local firefighters. You may also be able to get permission to sit in on some of the formal training classes for firefighters offered by city fire departments. In some cases, depending on the size and regulations of the town or city department, you may be able to gain experience by working as a volunteer firefighter.

"Many departments offer explorer and cadet programs for high-school age students to become involved in if they are interested in the fire service," notes Chief Bruegman. "There are classes that can be taken at local community colleges even by high school students to begin preparing them for a career in the fire service. Many departments offer programs that allow civilians to ride along. This is a good way for students to spend several hours in a fire station and actually respond to calls to get a feel for whether this is the career that is right for them. Also, any volunteer work, especially in service-related fields such as hospitals and hospices that provide services to people in need, would help prepare students for the jobs that firefighters do every day."

Courses in lifesaving and first aid will offer you experience in these aspects of the firefighter's job. You can explore these areas through community training courses and the training offered by the Boy Scouts of America or the American Red Cross. Individuals serving in the military may request training and assignment to fire-fighting units to gain experience.

EMPLOYERS

More than nine out of every 10 career firefighters work in municipal or county fire departments that protect 25,000 or more people. Some very large cities have several thousand firefighters, while small towns might only have a few. The remainder work in fire departments on federal and state installations, such as military bases, airports, and the U.S. Forestry Department. Private fire brigades employ a very small number of firefighters. Most volunteers work for departments that protect fewer than 25,000 people. More than half of all volunteer firefighters are located in small, rural departments that protect fewer than 9,999 people, according to the National Volunteer Fire

Council. Many industries have their own fire-protection staffs and private fire brigades.

STARTING OUT

You can enter this occupation by applying to take the local civil service examinations. This usually requires passing the physical health, physical performance, and written general intelligence examinations.

If you successfully pass all of the required tests and receive a job appointment, you may serve a probationary period during which you receive intensive training. After the completion of this training, you may be assigned to a fire department or engine company for specific duties.

In some small towns and communities, applicants may enter this occupation through on-the-job training as volunteer firefighters or by applying directly to the local government for the position.

ADVANCEMENT

Firefighters are generally promoted from within the department, first to the position of firefighter, first grade. After they demonstrate successful job performance and gain experience, firefighters may be promoted to positions as lieutenants, captains, deputies, battalion chiefs, assistant chiefs, deputy chiefs, and finally fire chief. Firefighters may sometimes work three to five years or more to receive a promotion to lieutenant. Promotions usually depend upon the firefighter's position rating, which is determined by seniority, job performance, and scores made on the periodic written examinations.

EARNINGS

The median hourly pay for firefighters was $18.80 in 2005 (or $39,090 annually based on a 40-hour workweek), according to the U.S. Department of Labor. Ten percent of all firefighters earned less than $9.49 (or $19,730 annually), while the top 10 percent earned more than $30.53 (or $63,510 annually). The department also reports that firefighters employed by local government earned a median hourly salary of $19.62 (or $40,810 annually) in 2005; those employed by the federal government earned a median hourly salary of $18.82 (or $39,140 annually) in 2005. Many firefighters receive longevity pay for each year they remain in service, which may add as much as $1,000 per year to their salaries. Firefighters also earn overtime pay and are usually given shift, weekend, and holiday pay differentials. In addition, firefighters generally

How to Become a Fire Chief by 30

Chief Bobby Williams, Spokane Fire Department, Spokane, Washington, shares his background and offers some insights on how to become a professional firefighter.

"I grew up in a small town in Chesterfield County, Virginia. My father owned a neighborhood grocery store across the street from the volunteer fire station. My dad became a volunteer shortly after opening the store and continued to do so for several years. My brother and I were at the fire station every chance we had. In our early teens, we would accompany our father on calls when he drove his own car to fire scenes.

"At 15, I became a junior firefighter and could do everything but drive the trucks. I fell in love with the fire service and knew right away that it was what I wanted to do professionally. At age 15, I set my goal to become a fire chief of a good-sized community before I was 30 years old.

"To meet that goal, I knew that I would need a formal education, so I attended Rowan Technical Institute in Salisbury, North Carolina, and obtained my degree in fire and safety engineering. During my seven quarters there, I was a resident firefighter. When I graduated, I worked as a paid firefighter for the Chesterfield Fire Department for one year. Then I went on to obtain a bachelor's degree in fire protection and a master's degree in business administration from Oklahoma State University.

"Students who are interested in this career need to understand the actual jobs that we perform in the fire service. Many folks are not aware that, for example, approximately 75 percent of our incidents are of an emergency medical nature. Talk to those who are doing the jobs to get a better idea of what is really involved. Visit your local fire department. Many work with their school districts to provide this opportunity. Investigate the possibility of becoming a resident firefighter. That experience can be helpful in obtaining career firefighting jobs.

"Next, make sure to research the best formal education programs that offer a major in fire protection. My high school guidance counselor and the local fire chief both encouraged me to go beyond the fire and safety engineering degree. They knew that employment as a fire chief would require those advanced degrees, and they were right."

receive a uniform allowance and are eligible to retire after 25 years of service or if disabled in the line of duty. Benefits, including health, life, and disability insurance, vary widely according to the community.

Fire lieutenants, captains, and fire chiefs earned salaries that ranged from $37,020 to $92,780 in 2005, according to the U.S. Department of Labor, although fire chiefs in larger cities may earn much more. Inspectors and investigators earned an average of $47,090 per year in 2005.

WORK ENVIRONMENT

The work of firefighters can often be exciting; the job, however, is one of grave responsibilities. Someone's life or death often hangs in the balance. The working conditions are frequently dangerous and involve risking one's life in many situations. Floors, walls, or even entire buildings can cave in on firefighters as they work to save lives and property in raging fires. Exposure to smoke, fumes, chemicals, and gases can end a firefighter's life or cause permanent injury.

"A typical day for a firefighter revolves around training, fire inspections, and house duties, including maintaining living quarters and equipment," says Chief Randy Bruegman. "Coupled with the typical day are untypical interruptions. This is what makes the life of a firefighter so interesting. When you place your turnout equipment [protective gear and clothing made of fire-resistant materials] on the apparatus you are assigned to, you never know what the day will bring. It can be a day filled with minor responses, typical medical assists, cardiac arrests, or multiple-alarm fires. I think that is what makes the job so challenging, as well as enjoyable. You never really know from one minute to the next what you might be doing."

New equipment that can make the firefighter's job much safer is constantly being developed and tested. For example, a company recently introduced special masks that allow firefighters to see in the dense and smoky environments they enter. These masks display heat sources close in temperature to the human body, allowing firefighters to locate victims in rooms otherwise impenetrable. With developments like these, firefighters will be able to save many more victims and drastically reduce the danger to them.

In many fire departments, firefighters may be on duty and live at fire stations for long periods of time. They may work 24-hour shifts followed by either 48 or 72 hours off. Firefighters can also work in split shifts, which require that they work nine-hour days and 15-hour night tours or 10-hour days and 14-hour night tours. After each set of day tours, firefighters receive 72 hours off, and after each set of night tours, they receive 48 hours off. Workweeks can range from 40 to almost 56 hours; across the United States and Canada, firefighters worked an average week of 50 hours.

This occupation requires a great deal of physical strength and stamina, so firefighters must work to keep themselves physically fit and in condition. They must be mentally alert at all times. Firefighters may be called into action at any time of the day or night and be required to work in all types of weather conditions, sometimes for long hours. Firefighters must do their work in a highly organized team effort to be effective, since a great deal of excitement and public confusion is usually present at the site of a fire.

Firefighters know that their work is essential for the public welfare, and they receive a great deal of personal satisfaction, as well as admiration and respect from society. "Firefighting is probably one of the few careers that taxes people both mentally and physically to their maximum potential on a daily basis," Chief Bruegman adds. "When responding to emergencies, firefighters are charged with taking a chaotic and stressful situation, gaining control of it, and trying to effect a positive outcome. That often happens within just a few minutes and requires an extreme amount of physical exertion and mental readiness."

OUTLOOK

Firefighting is forecasted to remain a very competitive field, and the number of people interested in becoming firefighters will outweigh the number of available positions in most areas. Employment of firefighters is expected to grow faster than the average for all occupations through 2014, according to the U.S. Department of Labor.

Most new jobs will be created as small communities grow and augment their volunteer staffs with career firefighters. There are also growing numbers of "call" firefighters, who are paid only when responding to fires. Little growth is expected in large, urban fire departments. Some local governments are expected to contract for firefighting services with private companies. In some fire departments, the hours of each work shift have been shortened, and two people may be employed to cover a shift normally worked by one person. Most job growth will occur as volunteer firefighting departments are converted to paid positions. Layoffs of firefighters are uncommon, given the essential nature of fire protection to communities.

FOR MORE INFORMATION

For news in the firefighting field, visit the IAFC's Web site.
International Association of Fire Chiefs (IAFC)
4025 Fair Ridge Drive, Suite 300
Fairfax, VA 22033-2868

Tel: 703-273-0911
http://www.iafc.org

The IAFF's Web site has a Virtual Academy with information on scholarships for postsecondary education.
International Association of Fire Fighters (IAFF)
1750 New York Avenue, NW
Washington, DC 20006-5301
Tel: 202-737-8484
http://www.iaff.org

For more information on certification, contact
International Fire Service Accreditation Congress
Oklahoma State University
1700 West Tyler
Stillwater, OK 74078-8075
Tel: 405-744-8303
Email: rhall@ifsac.org
http://www.ifsac.org

For information on fire safety issues, careers in fire protection, and public education, contact
National Fire Protection Association
One Batterymarch Park
Quincy, MA 02169-7471
Tel: 617-770-3000
Email: public_affairs@nfpa.org
http://www.nfpa.org

Forensic Experts

OVERVIEW

Forensic experts apply scientific principles and methods to the analysis, identification, and classification of physical evidence relating to criminal (or suspected criminal) cases. They do much of their work in laboratories, where they subject evidence to tests and then record the results. They may travel to crime scenes to collect evidence and record the physical facts of a site. Forensic experts may also be called upon to testify as expert witnesses and to present scientific findings in court.

HISTORY

In Scotland during the late 1780s, a man was convicted of murder when the soles of his boots matched a plaster cast of footprints taken from the scene of the crime. This is one of the earliest recorded cases of the use of physical evidence to link a suspected criminal with the crime.

In the late 19th century, scientists learned to analyze and classify poisons so their presence could be traced in a body. At about the same time, a controversy arose over the different methods being used to identify individuals positively. Fingerprinting emerged in the early 20th century as the most reliable method of personal identification. With the advent of X-ray technology, experts could rely on dental records to substitute for fingerprint analysis when a corpse was in advanced stages of decomposition and the condition of the skin had deteriorated.

Forensic pathology (medical examination of suspicious or unexplained deaths) also came into prominence at this time, as did ballistics, which is the study of projectiles and how they are shot from

QUICK FACTS

School Subjects
Biology
Chemistry

Personal Skills
Following instructions
Technical/scientific

Work Environment
Primarily indoors
Primarily multiple locations

Minimum Education Level
Bachelor's degree

Salary Range
$20,000 to $44,590 to $100,000+

Certification or Licensing
None available

Outlook
Faster than the average

DOT
188

GOE
04.03.02

NOC
N/A

O*NET-SOC
19-4092.00

firearms. The study of ballistics was aided by the invention of the comparison microscope, which enabled an investigator to look at bullets side by side and compare their individual markings. Since individual gun barrels "scar" bullets in a unique pattern, similar markings found on different bullets may prove that they were fired from the same weapon.

These investigations by pioneer forensic scientists led the courts and the police to acknowledge the value of scientifically examined physical evidence in establishing guilt or innocence, confirming identity, proving authenticity of documents, and establishing cause of death. As the result of this acceptance by the legal and law enforcement

Computer-Aided
Ballistics Identification

Spent bullets and cartridges, like fingerprints, are unique, each imprinted with striations, or markings, traceable to a single source. For this reason they are often the most telling pieces of evidence found at a crime scene; they are also the most complicated. In the past, it often took weeks, if not months, of comparative microscopic analysis before a firearms expert could link bullets and cartridges to their weapons of origin. Today, this process can take less than a day. How? Technological advances—in computers, networks, imaging devices, and microscopes, among other things—made possible the development of computer-aided ballistics identification. Today, this system, accessible to law enforcement agencies around the country, is known as the National Integrated Ballistic Information Network (NIBIN).

In 1992 the Federal Bureau of Investigation (FBI) implemented Drugfire, a computerized system that identified and stored information on gun cartridge cases that were recovered from crime scenes or from test fires of confiscated weapons. When a new casing was brought in for analysis, a firearms examiner added the casing's information to the Drugfire system by placing it on a microscope attached to a computer, which made a computerized image of the casing's breech face marks and firing pin impressions. The image information was committed to the system's databases, and the examiner then had the computer search for images of casings with similar markings already stored in the database. The computer then produced a short list of possible matches for the firearms expert to examine in detail. This process greatly reduced the time it took for examiners to analyze information by hand and determine matches. It also allowed firearms examiners to easily track a weapon and provide law enforcement communities, crime laboratories were established. One of the first, largest, and most complete laboratories is that of the Federal Bureau of Investigation (FBI), founded in 1932. Today, the FBI laboratory examines many thousands of pieces of evidence each year, and its employees present their findings in trials all over the United States and around the world. As the forensic sciences proved their worth, crime laboratories were established in larger cities and by state police departments. These laboratories are used in turn by many communities too small to support labs of their own. The scientific analysis of evidence has become an accepted part of police procedure, and new forensic advances, such as DNA testing, are being developed every day.

personnel with information on where and when that weapon had been used before.

At about the same time, the Bureau of Alcohol, Tobacco, Firearms, and Explosives (ATF) began exploring the possibility of using computers, networks, and other technologies to create a database of information on projectiles and cartridge casings from crime guns. To do this, the ATF began using the Integrated Ballistics Identification System (IBIS) in the mid-1990s. This system functioned in much the same way that Drugfire did, using microscope/computer units, databases, and networking. IBIS, however, was also able to incorporate information on severely damaged bullets as well as intact bullets and cartridge casings for matching purposes.

Although both Drugfire and IBIS proved to be excellent law enforcement tools, the two systems were not "interoperable"—that is, they couldn't share information. To bridge this gap, the FBI and ATF began to review and test new systems that would provide a single network, and the NIBIN was created to meet this need. In 2000, implementation of the NIBIN program began, with the ATF responsible for the field operations (including the purchasing of equipment and training of users) and the FBI responsible for the communications network.

Like the two previous systems, NIBIN does not make a positive match of bullets or casings from the same weapon. The system provides firearms examiners with a list of possible matches that they can compare to the physical evidence.

NIBIN has improved on both of these systems and become a powerful weapon used to solve violent crimes. Today, there are more than 926,000 pieces of crime scene evidence in the system, and thousands of matches, or "hits," have already occurred.

To read success stories involving NIBIN, visit http://www.nibin.gov/nb_success.htm.

THE JOB

Forensic experts, also called *criminalists*, use the instruments of science and engineering to examine physical evidence. They use spectroscopes, microscopes, gas chromatographs, infrared and ultraviolet light, microphotography, and other lab measuring and testing equipment to analyze fibers, fabric, dust, soils, paint chips, glass fragments, fire accelerants, paper and ink, and other substances in order to identify their composition and origin. They analyze poisons, drugs, and other substances found in bodies by examining tissue samples, stomach contents, and blood samples. They analyze and classify blood, blood alcohol, semen, hair, fingernails, teeth, human and animal bones and tissue, and other biological specimens. Using samples of the DNA in these materials, they can match a person with a sample of body tissue. They study documents to determine

Darrell Hall repackages drug evidence after weighing it and removing a sample for analysis at Oregon's state forensic lab. *(Greg Wahl-Stephens/ AP)*

whether they are forged or genuine. They also examine the physical properties of firearms, bullets, and explosives.

At the scene of a crime (whether actual or suspected), forensic experts collect and label evidence. This painstaking task may involve searching for spent bullets or bits of an exploded bomb and other objects scattered by an explosion. They might look for footprints, fingerprints, and tire tracks, which must be recorded or preserved by plaster casting before they are wiped out. Since crime scenes must eventually be cleaned up, forensic experts take notes and photographs to preserve the arrangement of objects, bodies, and debris. They are sometimes called on later to reconstruct the scene of a crime by making a floor plan or map pinpointing the exact location of bodies, weapons, and furniture.

One important discipline within forensic science is identification. *Fingerprint classifiers* catalog and compare fingerprints of suspected criminals with records to determine if the people who left the fingerprints at the scene of a crime were involved in previous crimes. They often try to match the fingerprints of unknown corpses with fingerprint records to establish their identities. They work in laboratories and offices, and travel to other areas such as crime scenes. Retrieving fingerprints outside may be difficult and require specialized processes, such as dusting glassware, windows, or walls with a fine powder. This powder contrasts with many different surfaces and will highlight any fingerprints that remain. Another method of retrieving fingerprints is to lift them off with a flexible tape, which can be brought back to the laboratory for further evaluation and matching.

Fingerprint classifiers compare new prints against those found after the commission of similar crimes. The classifier documents this information and transfers it to the main record-keeping system, often a large mainframe computer system. In the last decade or so, computers have greatly enhanced the possibility of matching new fingerprints to those already on file. A fingerprint classifier may keep individual files on current crimes and note any similarities between them.

Identification technicians work at various jobs related to maintaining police records. In addition to handling fingerprint records, they also work with other kinds of records, such as police reports and eyewitness information about crimes and accidents. They operate equipment used to microfilm police records, as well as store the microfilm and retrieve or copy records upon the request of police or other public officials. *Forensic pathologists* perform autopsies to determine the cause of death; autopsies are almost always performed on victims of crime. *Forensic psychiatrists* also conduct psychiatric evaluations of accused criminals and are often called to testify on whether the accused is mentally fit to stand trial.

Molecular biologists and *geneticists* analyze and review forensic and paternity samples, provide expert testimony in civil and criminal trials, and identify and develop new technologies for use in human identification.

Other job titles within forensic science include *forensic toxicologists,* who are concerned with detecting and identifying the presence of poisons or drugs in a victim's body; *forensic odontologists,* who use dental records and evidence to identify crime victims and to investigate bite marks; and *forensic anthropologists,* who examine and identify bones and skeletal remains.

Forensic experts spend the bulk of their time in the laboratory working with physical evidence. They seldom have direct contact with persons involved in actual or suspected crimes or with police investigators except when collecting evidence and reporting findings. Forensic experts do not interpret their findings relative to the criminal investigation in which they are involved; that is the work of police investigators. The purpose of crime lab work is to provide reliable, scientific analysis of evidence that can then be used in criminal investigations and, if needed later, in court proceedings.

REQUIREMENTS

High School

Almost all jobs in this field require at least a bachelor's degree. In high school, you can begin to prepare for a career in forensics by taking a heavy concentration of science courses, including chemistry, biology, physiology, and physics. Computer skills are also important, especially for fingerprint classifiers. A basic grounding in spoken and written communications will be useful because forensic experts must write very detailed reports and are sometimes called on to present their findings in court.

Postsecondary Training

A number of universities and community colleges in the United States offer programs in forensic science, pathology, and various aspects of crime lab work. These courses are often spread throughout the school, in the anatomy, physiology, chemistry, or biology departments, or they may be grouped together as part of the criminal justice department.

Certification or Licensing

Certification may be an advantage for people working in toxicology and document examination. Specialists in these and other disciplines may also be required to take undergraduate and graduate course work in their areas. In a field such as toxicology, advanced chemistry work is important.

Other Requirements
To be successful in this field, you should have an aptitude for scientific investigation, an inquiring and logical mind, and the ability to make precise measurements and observations. Patience and persistence are important qualities, as is a good memory. Forensic experts must constantly bear in mind that the accuracy of their lab investigations can have great consequences for others.

EXPLORING

A large community police department may have a crime lab of its own whose experts can give you specific information about their work and the preparation that helped them build their careers. Smaller communities often use the lab facilities of a larger city nearby or the state police. A school counselor or a representative of the local police may be able to help you arrange a tour of these labs. Lectures in forensic science given at universities or police conventions may also be open to students. Online services and Internet access may provide entry to forums devoted to forensic science and are good sources of information on the daily and professional experiences of people already active in this field.

EMPLOYERS

Forensic scientists are typically employed by large police departments or state law enforcement agencies nationwide. However, individuals in certain disciplines are often self-employed or work in the private sector. For example, large corporations, small firms, and government agencies may employ forensic engineers, who use mathematical principles to reconstruct accident scenes, determine the origins of explosions and fires, or review the design of chemical or molecular structures. Forensic anthropologists, who identify skeletal remains, may work within a university or college, teaching related courses, conducting research, and consulting on cases submitted by law enforcement agencies. They may also be employed by the military or a medical examiner's office. Many forensic science concentrations also offer part-time or consulting opportunities, depending on your level of education and experience.

STARTING OUT

Crime labs are maintained by the federal government and by state and local governments. Applications should be made directly to the personnel department of the government agency supporting the lab. Civil service appointments usually require applicants to take an examination. Such appointments are usually widely advertised well in advance of the application date. Those working for the FBI or other law enforcement agencies usually undergo background checks, which examine their character, background, previous employers, and family and friends.

ADVANCEMENT

In a large crime laboratory, forensic technicians usually advance from an assistant's position to working independently at one or more special types of analysis. From there, they may advance to a position as project leader or being in charge of all aspects of one particular investigation. In smaller labs, one technician may have to fill many roles. With experience, such a technician may progress to more responsible work but receive no advancement in title. Fingerprint classifiers who work for police departments may pursue advancement with a different government agency or apply for positions with the FBI.

Crucial to advancement is further education. Forensic experts need to be familiar with scientific procedures such as gas chromatography, ultraviolet and infrared spectrophotometry, mass spectroscopy, electrophoresis, polarizing microscopy, light microscopy, and conventional and isoelectric focusing; knowledge of these analytical techniques and procedures is taught or more fully explored at the master's and doctorate levels. Other, more specific areas of forensics, such as DNA analysis, require advanced degrees in molecular biology and genetics.

EARNINGS

Earnings for forensic analysts vary with the employer, geographic location, and educational and skill levels. Salaries for entry-level positions as research assistants or technicians working in local and regional labs range from $20,000 to $25,000. For those individuals with a bachelor's degree and two to five years of specialized experience, salaries range from $30,000 to $40,000. Salaries for those with advanced degrees range from $50,000 to well over $100,000 a year. The U.S. Department of Labor reports that the median hourly salary for forensic science technicians was $21.44 in 2005. For full-time employment, this means a median salary of approximately $44,590 a year.

WORK ENVIRONMENT

Forensic experts usually perform the analytical portion of their work in clean, quiet, air-conditioned laboratories, but they are frequently required to travel to crime scenes to collect evidence or study the site to understand more fully the evidence collected by detectives. When gathering evidence and analyzing it, forensic experts need to be able to concentrate, sometimes in crowded, noisy situations. For this reason, forensic experts must be adaptable and able to work in a variety of environments, including dangerous or unpleasant places.

Many crime scenes are grisly and may be extremely distressing for beginning workers and even for more seasoned professionals. In addition, forensic experts who work with human remains will regularly view corpses, and, more often than not, these corpses will have been mutilated in some way or be in varying degrees of decomposition. Individuals interested in this field need to develop the detachment and objectivity necessary to view corpses and extract specimens for testing and analysis.

Simulating the precise conditions of a crime site for a full analysis is often crucial, so forensic experts often return to the site so that they can perform tests or functions outside of the controlled environment of their lab. When traveling to the scene of a crime, forensic experts may have to carry cases of tools, cameras, and chemicals. In order not to risk contaminating evidence, they must follow strict procedures (both in and out of the laboratory) for collecting and testing evidence; these procedures can be extremely time-consuming and thus require a great deal of patience. Forensic experts also need to be able to arrive at and present their findings impartially. In large labs, they often work as part of a team under the direction of a senior technologist. They may experience eyestrain and contact with strong chemicals, but little heavy physical work is involved.

OUTLOOK

The number of forensic experts employed in the United States is expected to grow much faster than the average for all other occupations through 2014, according to the U.S. Department of Labor. Population increases, a rising crime rate, and the greater emphasis on scientific methodology in crime investigation have increased the need for trained experts. Forensic experts who are employed by state public safety departments should experience especially strong employment opportunities, although some government agencies may be under pressure to reduce staff because of budget problems. Forensic experts with a four-year degree in forensic science will enjoy the best employment prospects.

FOR MORE INFORMATION

For information careers and colleges and universities that offer forensic science programs, contact
American Academy of Forensic Sciences
410 North 21st Street
Colorado Springs, CO 80904-2798
Tel: 719-636-1100
http://www.aafs.org

To learn more about forensic services at the FBI, visit the FBI Laboratory Division's Web site.
Federal Bureau of Investigation (FBI)
J. Edgar Hoover Building
935 Pennsylvania Avenue, NW
Washington, DC 20535-0001
Tel: 202-324-3000
http://www.fbi.gov and http://www.fbi.gov/hq/lab/labhome.htm

For additional information on forensics and forensics professionals, contact the following organizations
American Society of Questioned Document Examiners
PO Box 18298
Long Beach, CA 90807-8298
http://www.asqde.org

Society of Forensic Toxicologists
One MacDonald Center
One North MacDonald Street, Suite 15
Mesa, AZ 85201-7339
Tel: 888-866-7638
http://www.soft-tox.org

Parole Officers

OVERVIEW

Parole is the conditional release of a prisoner who has not served out a full sentence. A long-standing practice of the U.S. justice system, parole is granted for a variety of reasons, including the "good behavior" of a prisoner, as well as overcrowding in prisons.

Prisoners on parole, or parolees, are assigned to a *parole officer* upon their release. It is the job of the parole officer to meet periodically with the parolee to ensure that the terms of the release are followed; to provide guidance and counseling; and to help the parolee find a job, housing, a therapist, or any other means of support. Parolees who break the release agreement may be returned to prison.

HISTORY

The use of parole can be traced at least as far back as the 18th century, when England, awash in the social currents of the Enlightenment and Rationalism, began to cast off its reliance on punishment by death. Retribution as the primary legal goal was increasingly challenged by the idea that reform of prisoners was not only possible but also desirable. At first, this new concern took the form of a conditional pardon from a death sentence. Instead of being executed, felons were sent away to England's foreign possessions, initially to the American colonies to fill their acute labor shortage. Although this practice actually began in the 1600s, it was not until the next century that a majority of condemned convicts were pardoned and transported across the ocean. After the American colonies gained independence in the late 18th century, England began to ship felons to Australia.

QUICK FACTS

School Subjects
Government
Psychology

Personal Skills
Helping/teaching
Leadership/management

Work Environment
Primarily indoors
One location with some
  travel

Minimum Education Level
Bachelor's degree

Salary Range
$27,600 to $40,210 to
  $67,440+

Certification or Licensing
Voluntary

Outlook
About as fast as the average

DOT
195

GOE
04.03.01

NOC
4155

O*NET-SOC
21-1092.00

An important next step in the history of parole is the "ticket of leave," first bestowed upon transported convicts in Australia. Taking various forms, this system eventually allowed a convict to be released from government labor but only after a designated number of years and only as a result of good conduct or behavior.

In the mid-19th century, the English Penal Servitude Act abolished the practice of transporting convicts to colonies and replaced it with the sentence of imprisonment. The use of the ticket of leave, however, was kept, and prisoners with good conduct could be freed after serving a designated part of the sentence. If the freed prisoner committed another crime, he or she would be required to complete the full term of the original sentence.

Although aspects of parole were tried as early as 1817 in New York state, a complete system of conditional and early release did not emerge in the United States until the 1870s. This program, begun in New York, included a method of grading prisoners, compulsory education, and supervision by volunteers called guardians, with whom the released prisoner was required to meet periodically. By 1916, every state and the District of Columbia had established a comparable program. This system of early release from prison came to be called *parole*—French for the word, promise, or speech—because prisoners were freed on their word, or parole, of honor.

Parole has been linked with the idea of rehabilitation since its beginning. Those on parole were given counseling and assistance in finding job training, education, and housing, but, unlike prisoners released without parole, they were also monitored. It was hoped that supervision, assistance, and the threat of being confined again would lessen the chance that released prisoners would commit another crime. Parole, however, has come to have other important functions. Releasing inmates who seem least likely to return to crime has commonly solved prison overcrowding. Inequities in sentencing have sometimes been corrected by granting early release to inmates with relatively long prison terms. Parole has also been used effectively as a means of disciplining disruptive prisoners while encouraging passive prisoners to good behavior. Without the incentive of parole, a prisoner would have to serve out the entire term of his or her sentence.

THE JOB

Parole officers play an important role in protecting society from crime. By helping, guiding, and supervising parolees, parole officers can reduce the chance that these individuals will again break the law and thus return to prison.

The regulations concerning parole differ from state to state. In some places, prisoners are given what are called indeterminate, or variable, sentences; if convicted of robbery, for example, an offender may be sentenced to no less than three years in prison but no more than seven. In this case, the prisoner would become eligible for parole after three years. In other places, an offender is given a definite sentence, such as seven years, but according to law may be paroled after completing a certain percentage of the sentence. Particularly heinous crimes may be excluded from the parole system.

Not all prisoners eligible for parole are released from prison. Parole is generally granted for good behavior, and those who successfully complete a drug or alcohol rehabilitation program, finish their GED (general equivalency diploma), or show other signs that they will lead a productive, crime-free life are considered good candidates for parole. In a few cases, such as prison overcrowding, prisoners might be released before they are technically eligible. A parole board or other government oversight committee makes the parole decision.

The work of a parole officer begins when a prisoner becomes eligible for parole. A parole officer working inside the correctional institution is given the job of writing a report on the prisoner. To help determine the risks involved in releasing the prisoner, the report might discuss the prisoner's family background, lifestyle before entering prison, personality, skills, and job prospects, as well as the crime for which the prisoner was incarcerated and any other crimes committed. The parole board or other oversight body reviews the report; conducts interviews with the prisoner, the prisoner's family, and others; and then decides whether the prisoner is suitable for release. In some cases, the parole officer might be called to testify or may help the prisoner prepare for the meeting with the parole board.

If released, the prisoner is assigned to another parole officer outside of the correctional institution. The initial meeting between the prisoner and this parole officer, however, may take place inside the prison, and it is there that the parole officer explains the legal conditions that the prisoner must follow. Beyond refraining from criminal activity, common conditions are attending school, performing community service, avoiding drug or alcohol abuse, not possessing a gun, and not associating with known criminals.

At this point, the parole officer tries not only to help the parolee find housing, employment, job training, or formal education but also to provide counseling, support, and advice. The parole officer may try to help by referring the parolee to other specialists, such as a psychologist or a drug rehabilitation counselor, or to a halfway house, where the parolee can live with other former prisoners and may be assisted by drug abuse counselors, psychologists, social workers, and other professionals. Parolees with financial problems may be referred to welfare agencies or social service organizations, and the parole officer may help arrange welfare or other public assistance. This is especially important for a parolee who has a family. The parole officer also sets up periodic meetings with the parolee.

An important part of the parole officer's job may be to contact and talk with businesses that might employ former prisoners. The parole officer tries to alleviate the concerns of business leaders reluctant to hire parolees and to highlight the role of the business community in helping former prisoners begin a new life.

Much of the parole officer's work is directed toward ensuring that the parolee is upholding the release agreement. The parole officer might interview the parolee's teachers, employers, or family and might conduct other types of investigations. Records must be kept of the parolee's employment or school status, finances, personal activities, and mental health. If the parolee does not follow the release agreement, the parole officer must begin proceedings for returning the parolee to a correctional institution. In some places, the parole officer is charged with arresting a parolee who is violating the agreement.

Parole officers often have a heavy caseload, and it is not unusual for 50 to 300 parolees to be assigned to a single parole officer. With so many parolees to monitor, little time may be spent on any single case. Some parole officers are helped by *parole aides* or *parole officer trainees*. A job with similar responsibilities is the *probation officer*, and some officers handle both parolees and those on probation. As the title suggests, probation officers work with offenders who are given probation, which is the conditional suspension of a prison sentence immediately after conviction. Probation is often given to first-time offenders. Like parolees, those on probation must follow strict guidelines, and failure to do so can result in incarceration. Probation officers, like parole officers, monitor the offenders; assist with finding employment, training, or education; make referrals to therapists and other specialists; help arrange public assistance; interview family, teachers, and employers; and provide advice and guidance. Those who work with children may be called *juvenile court workers*.

REQUIREMENTS

High School

If you are interested in this field, take a course load that provides adequate preparation for college studies. English, history, and the social sciences, as well as courses in civics, government, and psychol-

Learn More About It

Berson, Fred. *After the Big House: The True Adventures of a Parole Officer*. New York: Popular Library, 1953.

Jacobson, Michael. *Downsizing Prisons: How to Reduce Crime and End Mass Incarceration*. New York: New York University Press, 2006.

Keve, Paul W. *Prison, Probation, or Parole? A Probation Officer Reports*. Minneapolis, Minn.: University of Minnesota Press, 1954.

Learning Express. *Probation Officer/Parole Officer Exam*. New York: Learning Express, 2007.

National Learning Corporation. *Senior Parole Officer*. Syosset, N.Y.: National Learning Corporation, 2005.

Petersilia, Joan. *When Prisoners Come Home: Parole and Prisoner Reentry*. New York: Oxford University Press, 2003.

Rudman, Jack. *Parole Officer*. Syosset, N.Y.: National Learning Corporation, 2003.

Wilson, James Q., and Joan Petersilia. *Crime: Public Policies for Crime Control*. Oakland, Calif.: ICS Press, 2002.

ogy, are important subjects for high school students. Knowledge of a foreign language, particularly those spoken by larger immigrant and minority populations, will be especially helpful to a prospective parole officer. Some parole officer positions require fluency in specific foreign languages.

Postsecondary Training
The minimum educational requirement for becoming a parole officer is usually a bachelor's degree in criminal justice, criminology, corrections, social work, or a related subject. A degree in public administration, law, sociology, or psychology may also be accepted. A master's degree, as well as experience in social work or in a correctional institution, may be required for some positions.

Other Requirements
To be a successful parole officer, you should be patient, have good communications skills, and the ability to work well with and motivate other people.

EXPLORING

The best way to gain exposure to the field is to volunteer for a rehabilitation center or other social service organization. Some agencies offer internship programs for students interested in the field. It may also be helpful to call a local government agency handling parole and to arrange an informational interview with a parole officer.

EMPLOYERS

Most parole officers are employed by state or county correctional departments. Other parole officers are federal employees. Probation officers generally work for the courts. Halfway houses and work release centers also hire parole and probation officers. Approximately 93,000 workers are employed as probation officers and correctional treatment specialists in the United States.

STARTING OUT

After fulfilling the necessary requirements, many enter the field by directly contacting local civil service offices or county, state, or federal parole boards. In some areas, applicants are required to take a civil service examination. Job listings are also found in the placement offices of colleges and universities and in the classified section of newspapers. Contacts leading to employment are sometimes made during internships at a rehabilitation center or other organization. Greater opportunities exist for applicants with a master's degree and for those who are willing to relocate. Many parole officers are former police and corrections officers who have gained additional training.

ADVANCEMENT

Some people enter the field as a parole officer trainee before assuming the title of parole officer. New employees are given on-the-job training to learn the specifics of their job.

There are a number of higher level positions. Beyond the job of parole officer, there are opportunities as supervisors, administrators, and department heads. Some parole officers are promoted to director of a specialized unit.

EARNINGS

The U.S. Department of Labor reports that the median annual earnings for probation officers and correctional treatment specialists (the category under which parole officers are classified) were $40,210 in

2005. Salaries ranged from a low of less than $27,600 to $67,440 or more. Earnings vary by location and by level of government. Probation officers and correctional treatment specialists employed in state government earned a median salary of $44,590 in 2005, while those employed in local government earned $43,060. Educational level also affects salary. Parole officers who have advanced degrees generally earn more than those with only bachelor's degrees.

Like most government workers, parole officers receive a good benefits package. Benefits include vacation days, health insurance, and a pension plan.

WORK ENVIRONMENT

Parole officers usually work out of a clean, well-lighted office in a government building, courthouse, correctional institution, or social service agency. Those who work in the field must travel to various settings, such as private homes, businesses, or schools, in order to conduct interviews and investigations.

Parole officers typically have a 40-hour workweek, although overtime, as well as evening and weekend work, may be necessary. Because of potential emergencies, some may be on call 24 hours per day, seven days a week.

The job can bring a considerable amount of stress. Many parole officers have workloads that are too heavy, sometimes approaching 300 cases at once. Frustration over not having enough time to do an effective job is a common complaint. In addition, many parolees commit new crimes despite efforts by the parole officer to provide assistance. Others may be angry or violent and thus difficult to help or counsel. The job, in fact, can be dangerous. Despite the drawbacks, many people are attracted to the field and remain in it because they want to be challenged and because they know that their work has a positive impact on public safety.

OUTLOOK

The employment outlook for parole officers is good through 2014, according to the U.S. Department of Labor. The number of prisoners has increased dramatically during the past decade, and many will become eligible for parole. Overcrowding of prisons across the United States, combined with heightening concerns over the high cost of incarceration, have prompted the early release of many convicts who will require supervision. New programs replacing prison as a method of punishment and rehabilitation are being instituted in many states, and these programs will require additional parole officers. However, public outcry over perceived leniency toward convicted criminals, particularly repeat offenders, has created demand and even legislation for stiffer penalties and the withdrawal of the possibility of parole for many crimes. This development may ultimately decrease the demand for parole officers, as more and more criminals serve their full sentences.

FOR MORE INFORMATION

For industry information, contact
American Correctional Association (ACA)
206 North Washington Street, Suite 200
Alexandria, VA 22314-2528
Tel: 800-222-5646
http://www.aca.org

For information on probation and parole, contact
American Probation and Parole Association
2760 Research Park Drive
Lexington, KY 40511-8482
Tel: 859-244-8203
Email: appa@csg.org
http://www.appa-net.org

For a list of accredited bachelor's and master's degree programs in social work, contact
Council on Social Work Education
1725 Duke Street, Suite 500
Alexandria, VA 22314-3457
Tel: 703-683-8080
Email: info@cswe.org
http://www.cswe.org

For information on careers in social work, contact
National Association of Social Workers
750 First Street, NE, Suite 700
Washington, DC 20002-4241
Tel: 202-408-8600
http://www.naswdc.org

This Web site bills itself as "the Largest Online Community for Corrections."
The Corrections Connection
http://www.corrections.com

Police Officers

OVERVIEW

Police officers perform many duties relating to public safety. Their responsibilities include not only preserving the peace, preventing criminal acts, enforcing the law, investigating crimes, and arresting those who violate the law but also directing traffic, community relations work, and controlling crowds at public events. Police officers are employed at the federal, state, county, and city level.

State police officers patrol highways and enforce the laws and regulations that govern the use of those highways, in addition to performing general police work. Police officers are under oath to uphold the law 24 hours a day. There are approximately 842,000 police and detectives employed in the United States.

HISTORY

People have historically sought some form of protection for their lives and property and to help preserve their welfare. The true origins of police work, however, are virtually unknown. In medieval times, feudal lords employed retainers who made sure taxes were paid. These employees may have attempted to maintain some kind of law and order among the people, but at the same time, they were employed by the lords and often merely enforced their employers' wishes.

Colonial America followed the British form of police organization. A sheriff, appointed by the governor of a colony, enforced laws, collected taxes, and maintained public property throughout the colony. Constables performed similar duties in the cities and towns. Night watchmen protected the cities from fires and crime.

QUICK FACTS

School Subjects
Physical education
Psychology

Personal Skills
Communication/ideas
Leadership/management

Work Environment
Indoors and outdoors
Primarily multiple locations

Minimum Education Level
High school diploma

Salary Range
$27,150 to $46,290 to
  $88,570+

Certification or Licensing
None available

Outlook
About as fast as the average

DOT
375

GOE
04.03.01

NOC
6261

O*NET-SOC
33-3021.01, 33-3021.02,
  33-3051.00, 33-3051.01

However, as cities grew rapidly during the 19th century, a larger, more organized police service was needed to control growing problems with crimes and public disturbances.

This Idaho State Policeman talks on his radio while taking notes. *(Photo Researchers)*

In 1829 in London, Sir Robert Peel established the first modern, nonmilitary police force. The British police became known as *bobbies* after Sir Robert's name. The police force in New York City was established in 1844. These new police forces wore uniforms, worked 24 hours a day, and often carried guns. They patrolled the streets and soon became a fixture in many cities. On the American frontier, however, laws were often enforced by volunteer police officers until regular police forces were established. Sheriffs and sheriff's deputies guarded many areas of the West. An early effort to create a statewide police force resulted in the creation of the Texas Rangers in 1835. In 1905, Pennsylvania formed the first official state police department. Soon, almost every state had a state police department as well as police units that worked for individual cities or towns.

These early police efforts were often notoriously inadequate. Many police departments were seats of corruption and abuse of authority. Police officers were generally untrained and were often appointed as agents serving the political machine of their city, rather than the people. Efforts to clean up the police departments began in the early decades of the 20th century. Police were expected to be professionals. Higher selection standards and special training programs were instituted, and efforts were made to eliminate the influence of politics on the police department. Command of the police department soon became more centralized, with a chief of police supervising the operations of the entire department. Other ranks were created, such as sergeant and detective. At the same time, scientists working with the police were developing scientific advances in crime detection and prevention, such as fingerprinting.

Today, every state has uniformed police. State police operations are customarily confined to unincorporated areas as a matter of policy, although a few states restrict them by statute. In addition, police operate at the federal level in such agencies as the Federal Bureau of Investigation, the Immigration and Naturalization Service, and the Drug Enforcement Agency. While the many types of police forces operate independently, they often cooperate to provide more effective law enforcement.

THE JOB

Depending on the orders they receive from their commanding officers, police may direct traffic during the rush-hour periods and at special events when traffic is unusually heavy. They may patrol public places such as parks, streets, and public gatherings to maintain law and order. Police are sometimes called upon to prevent or break up riots and to act as escorts at funerals, parades, and other public events. They may administer first aid in emergency situations, assist in rescue operations of various kinds, investigate crimes, issue tickets to violators of traffic or parking laws or other regulations, or arrest drunk drivers. Officers in small towns may have to perform all of these duties and administrative work as well.

As officers patrol their assigned beats, either on foot, bicycle, horseback, motorcycle, or in cars, they must be alert for any situations that arise and be ready to take appropriate action. Many times they must be alert to identify stolen cars, identify and locate lost children, and identify and apprehend escaped criminals and others wanted by various law enforcement agencies. While on patrol, they keep in constant contact with headquarters and their fellow officers by calling in regularly on two-way radios. Although their profession may at times be dangerous, police officers are trained not to endanger their own lives or the lives of ordinary citizens. If they need assistance, they radio for additional officers.

In large city police departments, officers usually have more specific duties and specialized assignments. The police departments generally are comprised of special work divisions such as communications, criminal investigation, firearms identification, fingerprint identification and forensic science, accident prevention, and administrative services. In very large cities, police departments may have special work units such as the harbor patrol, canine corps, mounted police, vice squad, fraud or bank squad, traffic control, records control, and rescue units. A few of the job titles for these specialties are *identification and records commanders and officers, narcotics and vice detectives or investigators, homicide squad commanding officers, detective chiefs, traffic lieutenants, sergeants, parking enforcement officers, public safety officers, accident-prevention squad officers, safety instruction police officers,* and *community relations lieutenants.*

In very large city police departments, officers may fill positions as police chiefs, precinct sergeants and captains, desk officers, booking officers, police inspectors, identification officers, complaint evaluation supervisors and officers, and crime prevention police officers. Some officers work as plainclothes detectives in criminal investigation divisions. Internal affairs investigators are employed to police the police. Other specialized police officers include police commanding officers, who act as supervisors in missing persons and fugitive investigations; and officers who investigate and pursue nonpayment and fraud fugitives. Many police departments employ police clerks, who perform administrative and community-oriented tasks.

A major responsibility for state police officers (sometimes known as *state troopers* or *highway patrol officers*) is to patrol the highways and enforce the laws and regulations of those traveling on them. Riding in patrol cars equipped with two-way radios, they monitor traffic for troublesome or dangerous situations. They write traffic tickets and issue warnings to drivers who are violating traffic laws or otherwise not observing safe driving practices. They radio for assistance for drivers who are stopped because of breakdowns, flat tires, illnesses, or other reasons. They direct traffic around areas that are congested because of fires, road repairs, accidents, and other emergencies. They may check the weight of commercial vehicles to verify that they are within allowable limits, conduct driver examinations, or give safety information to the public.

In the case of a highway accident, officers take charge of the activities at the site by directing traffic, giving first aid to any injured parties, and calling for emergency equipment such as ambulances, fire trucks, or tow trucks. They write a report to be used by investigating officers who attempt to determine the cause of the accident.

In addition to these responsibilities, state police officers in most states do some general police work. They are often the primary law-enforcement agency in communities or counties that have no police force or a large sheriff's department. In those areas, they may investigate such crimes as burglary and assault. They also may assist municipal or county police in capturing lawbreakers or controlling civil disturbances.

Most police officers are trained in the use of firearms and carry guns. Police in special divisions, such as chemical analysis and handwriting and fingerprint identification, have special training to perform their work. Police officers often testify in court regarding cases with which they have been involved. Police personnel are required to complete accurate and thorough records of their cases.

REQUIREMENTS

High School

The majority of police departments today require that applicants have a high school education. Although a high school diploma is not always required, related work experience is generally required.

If you are interested in pursuing this career, you will find the subjects of psychology, sociology, English, law, mathematics, U.S. government and history, chemistry, and physics most helpful. Because physical stamina is very important in this work, sports and physical education are also valuable. Knowledge of a foreign language is especially helpful, and bilingual officers are often in great demand. If specialized and advanced positions in law enforcement interest you, pursue studies leading to college programs in criminology, criminal law, criminal psychology, or related areas.

Postsecondary Training

The best chance for advancement is by getting some postsecondary education, and many police departments now require a two- or four-year degree, especially for more specialized areas of police work. There are more than 800 junior colleges and universities offering two- and four-year degree programs in law enforcement, police science, and administration of justice. Many police departments require a two-year degree to make lieutenant and a bachelor's degree to make captain. The armed forces also offer training and opportunities in law enforcement that can be applied to civilian police work.

Newly recruited police officers must pass a special training program. After training, they are usually placed on a probationary period lasting from three to six months. In small towns and communities, a new officer may get his or her training on the job by working with an experienced officer. Inexperienced officers are never sent out on patrol alone but are always accompanied by veteran officers.

Large city police departments give classroom instruction in laws, accident investigation, city ordinances, and traffic control. These departments also give instruction in the handling of firearms, methods of apprehension and arrest, self-defense tactics, and first-aid techniques. Both state and municipal police officers are trained in safe driving procedures and maneuvering an automobile at high speeds.

Other Requirements

Police job appointments in most large cities and in many smaller cities and towns are governed by local civil service regulations. You will be required to pass written tests designed to measure your intelligence and general aptitude for police work. You will also be required to pass physical examinations, which usually include tests of physical agility, dexterity, and strength. Your personal history, background, and character will undergo careful scrutiny because honesty and law-abiding characteristics are essential traits for law-enforcement officers. Another important requirement is that you have no arrest record.

To be a police officer, you must be at least 20 years of age (or older for some departments), and some municipalities stipulate an age limit of not more than 35 years. You must have, in some cases, 20/20 uncorrected vision, good hearing, and weight proportionate to your height. You will also be required to meet locally prescribed weight and height rules for your gender. Most regulations require that you be a U.S. citizen, and many police departments have residency requirements.

If you hope to be a police officer, you should enjoy working with people and be able to cooperate with others. Because of the stressful nature of much police work, you must be able to think clearly and logically during emergency situations, have a strong degree of emotional control, and be capable of detaching yourself from incidents.

Physical fitness training is a mandatory, continuing activity in most police departments, as are routine physical examinations. Police officers can have no physical disabilities that would prevent them from carrying out their duties.

EXPLORING

A good way to explore police work is to talk with various law enforcement officers. Most departments have community outreach programs and many have recruiting programs as well. You may also wish to visit colleges offering programs in police work or write for information on their training programs.

In some cases, high school graduates can explore this occupation by seeking employment as police cadets in large city police departments. These cadets are paid employees who work part time in clerical and other duties. They attend training courses in police science on a part-time basis. When you reach the age of 21, you will be eligible to apply for regular police work. Some police departments also hire college students as interns.

EMPLOYERS

Police officers hold approximately 842,000 jobs in the United States. According to the U.S. Department of Labor, approximately 81 percent of police officers are employed by local governments. State police agencies employ approximately 12 percent of officers, and about 6 percent of officers work for federal agencies.

STARTING OUT

If you are interested in police work, you should apply directly to local civil service offices or examining boards to qualify as a candidate for police officer. In some locations, written examinations may be given to groups at specified times. For positions in smaller communities that do not follow civil service methods, you should apply directly to the police department or city government offices in that community.

If you are interested in becoming a state police officer, you can apply directly to the state civil service commission or the state police headquarters, which are usually located in the state capital.

ADVANCEMENT

Advancement in these occupations is determined by several factors. An officer's eligibility for promotion may depend on a specified length of service, job performance, formal education and training courses, and results of written examinations. Those who become eligible for promotion are listed on the promotional list along with other qualified candidates. Promotions generally become available from six months to three years after starting, depending on the department. As positions of different or higher rank become open, candidates are promoted to fill them according to their position on the list. Lines of promotion usually begin with officer third grade and progress to grade two and grade one. Other possible promotional opportunities include the ranks of detective, sergeant, lieutenant, or captain. Many promotions require additional training and testing. Advancement to the very top-ranking positions, such as division, bureau, or department director or chief, may be made by direct political appointment. Officers who have come up through the ranks hold most of these top positions.

Large city police departments offer the greatest number of advancement opportunities. Most of the larger departments maintain separate divisions, which require administration workers, line officers, and more employees in general at each rank level. Officers may move into areas that they find challenging, such as criminal investigation or forensics.

Most city police departments offer various types of in-service study and training programs. These programs allow police departments to keep up-to-date on the latest police science techniques and are often required for those who want to be considered for promotion. Police academies, colleges, and other educational institutions provide training courses. Some of the subjects offered are civil defense, foreign languages, and forgery detection. Some municipal police departments share the cost with their officers or pay all educational expenses if the officers are willing to work toward a college degree in either police work or police administration. Independent study is also often required.

The National Academy of the Federal Bureau of Investigation in Washington, D.C., offers intensive 12-week administrative courses for which a limited number of officers are selected to participate.

Advancement opportunities on police forces in small communities are considerably more limited by the rank and number of police personnel needed. Other opportunities for advancement may be found in related police, protective, and security service work with private companies, state and county agencies, and other institutions.

EARNINGS

According to the U.S. Department of Labor, police officers earned an annual average salary of $46,290 in 2005; the lowest 10 percent earned less than $27,150 a year, while the highest 10 percent earned $70,330 or more annually. Police detectives earned median salaries of $55,790 a year in 2005, with a low of less than $32,920 and a high of more than $88,570. Salaries for police officers range widely based on geographic location. Police departments in the West and North generally pay more than those in the South.

Most police officers receive periodic and annual salary increases up to a limit set for their rank and length of service. Police departments generally pay special compensation to cover the cost of uniforms, and they usually provide any equipment required such as firearms and handcuffs. Overtime pay may be given for certain work shifts or emergency duty. In these instances, officers are usually paid straight or time-and-a-half pay, while extra time off is sometimes given as compensation.

Because most police officers are civil service employees, they receive generous benefits, including health insurance and paid vacation and sick leave, and enjoy increased job security. In addition, most police departments offer retirement plans and retirement after 20 or 25 years of service, usually at half pay.

WORK ENVIRONMENT

Police officers work under many different types of circumstances. Much of their work may be performed outdoors, as they ride in patrol cars or walk the beats assigned to them. In emergency situations, no consideration can be made for weather conditions, time of day or night, or day of the week. Police officers may be on call 24 hours a day; even when they are not on duty, they are usually required by law to respond to emergencies or criminal activity. Although they are assigned regular work hours, individuals in police work must be willing to live by an unpredictable and often erratic work schedule. The work demands constant mental and physical alertness as well as great physical strength and stamina.

Police work generally consists of an eight-hour day and a five-day week, but police officers may work night and weekend shifts and on holidays. Emergencies may add many extra hours to an officer's day or week. The occupation is considered dangerous. Some officers are killed or wounded while performing their duties. Their work can involve unpleasant duties and expose them to sordid, depressing, or dangerous situations. They may be called on to deal with all types of people under many types of circumstances. While the routine of some assigned duties may become boring, the dangers of police work are often stressful for the officers and their families. Police work in general holds the potential for the unknown and unexpected, and most people who pursue this work have a strong passion for and commitment to police work.

OUTLOOK

Employment of police officers and detectives is expected to increase about as fast as the average for all occupations through 2014, according to the U.S. Department of Labor. Strong competition for jobs will exist at the federal level and in most state police departments. Opportunities will be best in local police departments, especially those which are located in high-crime areas or that offer relatively lower pay than other departments.

The opportunities that become available, however, may be affected by technological, scientific, and other changes occurring today in police work. Automation in traffic control is limiting the number of officers needed in this area, while the increasing reliance on computers throughout society is creating demands for new kinds of police work. New approaches in social science and psychological research are also changing the methodology used in working with public offenders. These trends indicate a future demand for more educated, specialized personnel.

This occupation has a very low turnover rate, but new positions will open as current officers retire, leave the force, or move into higher positions. Retirement ages are relatively low in police work compared to other occupations. Many officers retire while in their 40s and then pursue a second career. In response to increasing crime rates and threats of terrorism, some police departments across the country are expanding the number of patrol officers, although budget problems faced by many municipalities may limit growth.

In the past decade, private security firms have begun to take over some police activities such as patrolling public places. Some private companies have even been contracted to provide police forces for

Learn More About It

Baker, Barry M. *Becoming a Police Officer: An Insider's Guide to a Career in Law Enforcement*. Lincoln, Neb.: iUniverse, 2006.

Douglas, John. *John Douglas's Guide to Landing a Career in Law Enforcement*. New York: McGraw-Hill, 2004.

Hennessy, Stephen M. *Thinking Cop, Feeling Cop: A Study in Police Personalities*. New York: Center for Applications of Psychological Type, 1998.

Hesalroad, Mary. *Law Enforcement Career Starter*. 2d ed. New York, N.Y.: LearningExpress, 2001.

Stinchcomb, James. *Opportunities in Law Enforcement and Criminal Justice Careers*. 2d ed. New York: McGraw-Hill, 2002.

Sutton, Randy, and Cassie Wells. *True Blue: Police Stories by Those Who Have Lived Them*. New York: St. Martin's Press, 2004.

Wells, Sandra K., and Betty L. Alt. *Police Women: Life with the Badge*. Westport, Conn.: Praeger Publishers, 2005.

some cities. Many companies and universities also operate their own police forces.

FOR MORE INFORMATION

Created by the American Federation of Police and Concerned Citizens and the National Association of Chiefs of Police, the American Police Hall of Fame and Museum offers summer camps, scholarships, and other information for young people interested in police work.

American Police Hall of Fame and Museum
6350 Horizon Drive
Titusville, FL 32780-8002
Tel: 321-264-0911
Email: policeinfo@aphf.org
http://www.aphf.org

The National Association of Police Organizations is a coalition of police unions and associations that work to advance the interests of law enforcement officers through legislation, political action, and education.

National Association of Police Organizations
750 First Street, NE, Suite 920
Washington, DC 20002-8005
Tel: 202-842-4420
Email: info@napo.org
http://www.napo.org

INTERVIEW

Officer Steve Leuve is a member of the nationally renowned New York Police Department.

Q. Where do you work?
A. I'm a police officer in the 73rd Precinct in Brooklyn, New York. I've been on the job for a year now.

Q. Why did you want to be a police officer?
A. I always wanted to work in law enforcement. A couple of my cousins are in law enforcement, also, and hearing about their work got me even more interested.

Q. What is your educational background?
A. I have a high school diploma, and went to college for three and a half years. To work as a police officer for the city [New York], you need 60 college credits and a 2.0 GPA.

Q. What do you like most about the job?
A. I feel good about what I'm doing. I feel like I'm helping to better the community by making sure laws are obeyed.

Q. What's the hardest part of the job?
A. I work in a poor neighborhood, so it's really hard seeing how people live. It's hard seeing people hurt each other and seeing the arguments. Dealing with that every day is tough. It helps to keep a balance and try to get away from that outside of work. To relieve stress, I go to the gym, and spend time with my girlfriend, family, or friends who aren't in law enforcement.

Q. What advice do you have for students who are interested in becoming a police officer?
A. It's a great job. If you have an interest in law enforcement, train to become a police officer. You learn a lot while on the job, you can help improve communities, and you feel good about the work you are doing.

Process Servers

OVERVIEW

Process servers are licensed by the courts to serve legal papers, such as summonses, subpoenas, and court orders, to the parties involved in legal disputes. People served may include witnesses, defendants in lawsuits, or the employers of workers whose wages are being garnished by court order. Corporations can be served through their statutory agents (representatives), and unknown parties can be served as John or Jane Doe, with their true names being substituted when learned by the court. Process servers work independently or as employees of law firms and other companies.

HISTORY

Modern-day process servers owe their lineage to the English bailiff, whose powers included the serving and enforcement of common law decrees such as writs of attainder (a notice of outlawry, the loss of civil rights, or sentence of death), or habeas corpus (a call for one in custody to be brought to court). The bailiff was considered a minor court official with authority to serve the court in several ways, one of which included handling legal documents. In English literature, the most notable characterizations of bailiffs can be found in the works of the 19th-century writer Charles Dickens.

In the United States, constables carried out these duties until the 1930s, when the term *private process server* was coined to describe an official who could serve legal documents, but who had no law enforcement powers. The heavy burden of serving all the legal papers fell on the court officials and law enforcement personnel until the process server position was born. Although many sheriffs'

QUICK FACTS

School Subjects
English
Government

Personal Skills
Following instructions

Work Environment
Indoors and outdoors
Primarily multiple locations

Minimum Education Level
High school diploma

Salary Range
$14,330 to $20,870 to
$33,670+

Certification or Licensing
Recommended

Outlook
About as fast as the average

DOT
249

GOE
09.08.01

NOC
1227

O*NET-SOC
N/A

and marshals' offices carry out all criminal process service, independent process servers handle much of the civil process service.

THE JOB

Process servers are responsible for assuring that people are notified in a timely and legal fashion that they are required to appear in court. Their clients may include attorneys, government agencies (such as a state's attorney general's office), or any person who files a lawsuit, seeks a divorce, or begins a legal action. As private individuals, process servers occupy a unique position in the legal system: they are court officers, but not court employees; they cannot give legal advice, or practice as attorneys.

A process server's duties are also distinct from that of the sheriff's because process servers serve papers only in civil matters, although the sheriff and constable serve in both civil and criminal matters. Criminal arrest warrants, for example, or papers ordering the seizure of property, are served exclusively by sheriffs, constables, and other law enforcement officials. To ensure that private process servers aren't mistaken for law enforcement officials, most jurisdictions forbid process servers to wear uniforms and badges or to place official-looking emblems on their vehicles.

Process servers use their knowledge of the rules of civil procedure on a daily basis as they carry out their duties. Certain types of papers—for example, a summons or court orders—expire if not served within a certain number of days. Others, such as subpoenas, must be served quickly to allow a witness time to plan or to make travel arrangements. Eviction notices and notices of trustee sales can be posted on the property in certain situations, and writs of garnishments (orders to bring property to the court) require the process server to mail papers as well as serve them.

Besides being aware of the time limits on serving a paper, process servers must know whom they are allowed to serve in a given situation. A summons, for example, can be served directly to the person named or to a resident of the household, provided they are of a suitable age. A court order or a subpoena, on the other hand, can only be served to the person named. Special circumstances also exist for serving minors, people judged to be mentally incompetent, or people who have declared bankruptcy. Many such rules and exceptions exist, and the process server is responsible for making sure that every service is valid by following these rules. An invalid service can cause excessive delays in a case, or even cause a case to be dismissed due to procedural mistakes on the part of the process server. In light of this, many process servers, or the companies they work for, are bonded and carry malpractice insurance.

A process server's job is further complicated by the fact that many people do not want to be served and go to great lengths to avoid it. Much of a process server's time is spent skip-tracing—that is, attempting to locate an address for a person who has moved or who may be avoiding service. The client may provide the process server with some information about the person, such as a last known address, a place of business, or even a photograph of the person, but occasionally process servers have to gather much of this information on their own. Questioning neighbors or coworkers is a common practice, as is using the public information provided by government offices such as the assessor's office, voter's registration, or the court clerk to locate the person. Sometimes, process servers even stake out a home or business to serve papers.

Tony Klein, from the Process Server Institute, says the clientele and the people who are served vary according to the type of work the process server does. "Some servers have clients that send primarily collection lawsuits. The defendants are generally of low to moderate income, live in low- to moderate-income neighborhoods, and might be evasive. Some servers specialize in the high end, same day, special-handling assignments involving lawsuits over substantial amounts of money."

The actual service of the paper is a simple, often anticlimactic process. The process server identifies himself or herself as an officer of the court and tells the person that he or she is being served, then hands the person the documents. If the person won't accept service, or won't confirm his or her identity, the process server will drop papers or simply leave the documents. In the eyes of the court, the person is considered served whether or not they actually touch the papers, sign for them, or even acknowledge the process server's presence.

REQUIREMENTS

High School
If process serving sounds interesting to you, get a head start now and take courses in English, political science, communication, and any law or business-related courses. Training in a foreign language can also be extremely helpful because process servers may encounter non-English speakers.

Postsecondary Training
Although college is not required, advanced courses in psychology, communication, and business would be of great benefit to a

potential process server. You won't find many, if any, college or university majors called process serving; however, any college-level work in legal studies will prepare you for work in this field. The Process Server Institute (see their contact information at the end of this article) holds training seminars that focuses directly on process serving. This type of specific training will help a new process server more than the general legal studies approach.

Certification or Licensing
Any U.S. citizen who is not party to the case, is over the age of 18, and who resides in the state where the matter is to be tried may serve due process (that is, be a process server for a specific legal matter). However, people who serve papers on a regular basis usually must register with their particular state. The courts take the licensing of process servers seriously, and many jurisdictions require applicants to take a written exam; some even require an interview with the presiding judge. Alvin Esper, a process server in Indiana, recommends that all new servers obtain private detective status with their particular state: "This is not a requirement in most states or the federal courts," Esper adds, "but it can protect you when you must perform stakeouts to locate a person to be served." Because most states differ on their requirements, you should get more information from your local office of the Clerk of the Superior Court.

Other Requirements
Because process serving is a face-to-face job, people who excel in this field are usually bold, confident, and skilled at working with people. Gaining a reputation as reliable and responsible will go a long way with prospective clients who want someone who won't give up on serving papers to people. Because process servers often serve papers to people who don't want them, a certain element of danger is involved. Process servers must be willing to take that risk in some situations. Esper says, "Depending on the individual to be served, serving can be dangerous. I usually try to serve papers during daylight hours, depending on whether the neighborhood seems safe or unsafe."

EXPLORING
Check the National Association of Professional Process Servers Web site (http://www.napps.org) for process servers in your state. Contact some of these people who are working in the field now and

ask for information. Speaking to attorneys, or to a local constable or sheriff's deputy, can also be helpful. Since most court records are public, you can look at actual files of court cases to familiarize yourself with the types of papers served and examine affidavits filed by process servers.

EMPLOYERS

Most process servers are independent contractors. They set up their own service business and provide process serving to individuals, lawyers, and courts. Other process servers may work for small law firms, attorney's offices, or law enforcement agencies on a full-time or part-time basis. Because courts are located throughout the country, process servers will find opportunities just about everywhere. Larger cities will have more opportunities, of course, simply due to the higher concentration of people.

STARTING OUT

Most process serving companies train their new employees and encourage them to travel with licensed process servers to familiarize them with the job. Often, the employer will assist in preparing the employee for the examination by providing them with copies of the local rules or even a study guide. Because of the flexible hours and hands-on experience with legal papers and cases, process serving is a popular job with college students, especially those who are interested in becoming attorneys themselves.

Firms specializing in attorney services will frequently train messengers and other office personnel as process servers, because they are already familiar with legal terms and documents.

You won't see many advertisements in newspapers for process servers. Instead, the key to landing this job is to network with people in the legal profession. If you or someone in your family knows a lawyer, ask him or her to refer you to someone who may be interested in training a new process server.

ADVANCEMENT

A process server may start out as a legal messenger, delivering documents to law offices and filing papers with the city, state, or federal courts. In most jurisdictions, subpoenas don't need to be served by a licensed process server, so an employee of an attorney service can begin a career in process serving in this manner.

Words to Know

Affidavit: Written statement made under oath to an officer of the court.

Ex parte: On behalf of.

Garnishment: An order of the court that calls for the served person to bring certain property before the court.

Injunction: A judge's ruling to stop someone from doing something.

Process: A formal writing issued by authority of law.

Subpoena: A writ authorized by the court demanding that a witness appear in court.

Once licensed, a process server can expect to work for a firm as either a salaried employee or a private contractor. As process servers gain experience, they typically serve more papers, and perhaps acquire bigger or more lucrative territory in which to work. In this way, advancement is also tied to the papers themselves.

In a sense, the papers that a process server delivers or serves are actually worth money, but only to the process server who delivers them. Just as private delivery companies charge for their services, process serving companies or individuals also charge for their services. The difference is that the rates are determined by the courts, with the amount any given paper is worth legally fixed by law. Usually, the pricing is set in terms of the location of the delivery, the number of miles from the courthouse, and so on, but anything that makes delivery more difficult or time-consuming can add to the cost. For example, papers to be served to someone living 50 miles from the courthouse are worth more because it takes more time and money to drive 50 miles out of town. The value of those particular papers increases if they must be served within a day and the person being served has moved, forcing the process server to spend considerable time, money, and effort learning the new address. Because most process servers are independent contractors, they are rewarded for their seniority and long service with a company by being assigned to the most lucrative territories, or those areas in which the papers are worth the most.

Some process servers use the knowledge and experience they gain working for a firm to start their own businesses. Process servers who operate their own companies are responsible for all aspects of the business, from supervising and training personnel to advertising, accounting, and tax preparation.

EARNINGS

Earnings for process servers vary according to the number and type of papers served. If a process server is working as an employee of a firm, or as a private contractor, he or she can expect to earn approximately 25 to 40 percent of the total amount the firm charges the client to serve the paper. The average cost a firm charges to serve a paper is $25, but this number can vary wildly, depending on the mileage traveled to serve the paper, the number of attempts made, or any special efforts required to effect service. When taking into consideration skip-tracing, stakeout time, and other investigative efforts, the fee can be much higher.

A salaried employee who works part time as a process server can expect to make approximately $27,000, although a salaried, full-time process server can expect almost twice as much, approximately $45,000 to $50,000. The U.S. Department of Labor reports a median annual salary of $20,870 in 2005 for couriers and messengers, which includes those working for legal services. Earnings ranged from less than $14,330 to $33,670 or more. These figures can be misleading, however. A process server can work all day and not serve any papers. The next day, he or she could make almost $600. A non-salaried process server who hustles and has a decent territory can make good money, too. "The rate depends on the type of work and the need for it," Tony Klein says. "You can make a living doing this type of work. If you work for someone, you make less than working for yourself. Every market is different; for example, in California, independent servers make $2,000 to $4,000 per month."

Employees may receive such benefits as health insurance and paid vacation time.

WORK ENVIRONMENT

Being a process server requires a certain amount of hustle. The job requires that the person be part investigator, part process server, and part legal messenger. The successful process server will enjoy the more tedious aspects of sleuthing, such as tracking down routine information about someone's life.

Considering the process server's position as the bearer of bad news, it is not surprising that the job can be stressful at times. Defendants who have been avoiding service may become angry when finally served. Violence against process servers is rare but does occur. Subsequently, process servers need to remain clearheaded in stressful situations and be able to use their communication skills to their best advantage.

Process servers may work at any hour of the day in most jurisdictions, and many choose to work weekends or holidays as well. This allows for an extremely flexible work schedule, because the process server is usually the one who decides when to attempt service on a given paper. In scheduling an attempted service, the process server's main considerations are serving the paper as quickly as possible with the fewest number of attempts; if the party is not home, the process server must return later.

Many large, process serving companies assign their employees fixed areas to work in, allowing a process server to become familiar with a certain section of a large city, for example, or several small towns in a given area. Even if a process server has a fixed territory, he or she can still expect to travel to a wide variety of locations. "Process serving is a lot of driving," Esper says. "Most often, you are searching for the address of the person to be served." In the course of a year, a process server might serve at hospitals, prisons, schools, and any number of private offices.

When not serving papers, process servers spend much of their time working closely with attorneys, judges, and other court personnel. For this reason, many process servers dress in a professional manner. When serving, however, a process server may wear whatever he or she prefers, and many choose to dress casually. Some dress casually to appear unobtrusive, hoping that potentially evasive parties will be caught off guard, and therefore served more easily.

OUTLOOK

Employment opportunities for process servers will grow as the number of legal matters increases. The rising number of civil lawsuits bodes well for process servers, since a single case can produce anywhere from one service to dozens, when taking into account subpoenas, supporting orders, writs of garnishment, and the like.

Some sheriff's departments (long mandated by law to serve civil papers) are now beginning to rely solely on private process servers, because they cannot effectively compete with the faster and more inexpensive private process serving companies. Other jurisdictions, increasingly under pressure to justify serving civil papers at a loss, are likely to revise their laws as well.

From time to time, various jurisdictions experiment with service by registered mail, but these experiments are limited and usually not long-lasting, since the most efficient way to ensure that a person has been notified is to notify him or her in person.

FOR MORE INFORMATION

To learn more about membership, contact
National Association of Professional Process Servers
PO Box 4547
Portland, OR 97208-4547
Tel: 503-222-4180
Email: administrator@napps.org
http://www.napps.org

For information about training seminars, contact
Process Server Institute
667 Folsom Street, 2nd Floor
San Francisco, CA 94107-1314
Tel: 415-495-3850
Email: psinstitute@juno.com
http://www.psinstitute.com

For a listing of current process servers, contact
United States Process Servers Association
PO Box 19767
St. Louis, MO 63144-0167
Tel: 866-367-2841
Email: info@processservers.com
http://www.usprocessservers.com/home.htm

Secret Service Special Agents

QUICK FACTS

School Subjects
English
Foreign language
Physical education

Personal Skills
Communication/ideas
Helping/teaching

Work Environment
Indoors and outdoors
Primarily multiple locations

Minimum Education Level
Bachelor's degree

Salary Range
$25,195 to $55,360 to
$150,000+

Certification or Licensing
None available

Outlook
About as fast as the average

DOT
375

GOE
04.03.01

NOC
6261

O*NET-SOC
33-3021.03

OVERVIEW

Secret Service special agents are employed by the U.S. Secret Service, which is part of the Department of Homeland Security. Secret Service agents work to protect the president and other political leaders of the United States, as well as heads of foreign states or governments when they are visiting the United States. Special agents also investigate financial crimes. The U.S. Secret Service employs about 5,000 people, of which about 2,100 agents.

HISTORY

The Secret Service was established in 1865 to suppress the counterfeiting of U.S. currency. After the assassination of President William McKinley in 1901, the Secret Service was directed by Congress to protect the president of the United States. Today, it is the Secret Service's responsibility to protect the following people: the president and vice president (also president-elect and vice president-elect) and their immediate families; former presidents and their spouses for 10 years after the president leaves office (spouses lose protection if they remarry; all former presidents up to and including President Clinton receive lifetime protection, as this law changed in 1997); children of former presidents until they are 16 years old; visiting heads of foreign states or governments and their spouses traveling with them, along with other distinguished foreign visitors to the United States and their spouses traveling with them; official representatives of the United States who are performing special missions abroad; major presidential and vice-presidential candidates and, within 120 days of the general presidential election, their spouses.

THE JOB

Secret Service special agents are charged with two missions: protecting U.S. leaders or visiting foreign dignitaries (likewise, U.S. leaders on missions to other countries) and investigating the counterfeiting of U.S. currency. Special agents are empowered to carry and use firearms, execute warrants, and make arrests.

When assigned to a permanent protection duty—for the president, for example—special agents are usually assigned to the Washington, D.C., area. They are responsible for planning and executing protective operations for those whom they protect at all times. Agents can also be assigned to a temporary protective duty to provide protection for candidates or visiting foreign dignitaries. In either case, an advance team of special agents surveys each site that will be visited by those whom they protect. Based on their survey, the team determines how much manpower and what types of equipment are needed to provide protection. They identify hospitals and evacuation routes and work closely with local police, fire, and rescue units to develop the protection plan and determine emergency routes and procedures, should the need arise. A command post is then set up with secure communications to act as the communication center for protective activities. The post monitors emergencies and keeps participants in contact with each other.

Before the officials arrive, the *lead advance agent* coordinates all law enforcement representatives participating in the visit. The assistance of military, federal, state, county, and local law enforcement organizations is a vital part of the entire security operation. Personnel are told where they will be posted and are alerted to specific problems associated with the visit. Intelligence information is discussed and emergency measures are outlined. Just prior to the arrival of those whom they protect, checkpoints are established and access to the secure area is limited. After the visit, special agents analyze every step of the protective operation, record unusual incidents, and suggest improvements for future operations.

Protective research is an important part of all security operations. *Protective research engineers* and *protective research technicians* develop, test, and maintain technical devices and equipment needed to provide a safe environment for their charge.

Secret Service agents stand among tractors at the Iowa State Fair as they guard President Bush during his speech in 2002. *(Ken Lambert/AP)*

When assigned to an investigative duty, special agents investigate threats against those the Secret Service protects. They also work to detect and arrest people committing any offense relating to coins, currency, stamps, government bonds, checks, credit card fraud, computer fraud, false identification crimes, and other obligations or securities of the United States. Special agents also investigate violations of the Federal Deposit Insurance Act, the Federal Land Bank Act, and the Government Losses in Shipment Act. Special agents assigned to an investigative duty usually work in one of the Secret Service's 125 domestic and foreign field offices. Agents assigned to investigative duties in a field office are often called out to serve on a temporary protective operation.

Special agents assigned to investigate financial crimes may also be assigned to one of the Secret Service's three divisions in Washington, D.C., or they may receive help from the divisions while conducting an investigation from a field office. The Counterfeit Division constantly reviews the latest reprographic and lithographic technologies to keep a step ahead of counterfeiters. The Financial Crimes Division aids special agents in their investigation of electronic crimes involving credit cards, computers, cellular and regular telephones, narcotics, illegal firearms trafficking, homicide, and other crimes. The Forensic Services Division coordinates forensic science activities within the Secret Service. The division analyzes evidence such as documents, fingerprints, photographs, and video and audio recordings.

The Secret Service employs a number of specialist positions such as *electronics engineers, communications technicians, research psychologists, computer experts, armorers, intelligence analysts, polygraph examiners, forensic experts, security specialists,* and more.

For some 15 years, Norm Jarvis has been a special agent for the Secret Service. He has protected a variety of U.S. political leaders including former presidents Clinton, Nixon, Carter, and Ford. He has also protected foreign dignitaries including the president of Sudan and the prime minister of Israel. In addition, Jarvis has investigated criminal activity in a number of cities and served in the Secret Service's Montana and Utah field offices.

While his primary responsibility is to investigate crimes, Jarvis is called out regularly to protect a political or foreign leader. During those times, he serves as a member of a team of special agents who work to ensure there is always a "protective bubble," a 360-degree virtual boundary of safety, surrounding the person they are protecting, regardless of whether he or she is in a moving or stationary location. Protective operations can be complicated, with special agents working together around the clock, using intelligence and special technologies, and working in conjunction with local authorities to make sure the person is safe. "We don't believe anybody can do bodyguard work just by walking around with somebody," Jarvis says. "Scowls and large muscles don't mean a lot if somebody is determined to kill you." While special agents don't change their protective techniques when they work overseas, they often work in conjunction with foreign security agencies. "Other security forces usually defer to the Secret Service, which is considered a premier security agency," Jarvis says.

When Jarvis is not on a protective assignment, he spends his time investigating a variety of crimes. Special agents assigned to smaller field offices typically handle a wide variety of criminal investigations. But special agents usually work for a specialized squad in a field office, handling specific investigations like counterfeit currency, forgery, and financial crimes. Special agents may receive case referrals from the Secret Service headquarters, from other law enforcement agencies, or through their own investigations. Investigating counterfeit money requires extensive undercover operations and surveillance. Special agents usually work with the U.S. Attorney's Office and local law enforcement for counterfeiting cases. Through their work, special agents detect and seize millions of dollars of counterfeit money each year—some of which is produced overseas. Special agents working in a fraud squad often receive complaints or referrals from banking or financial institutions that have been defrauded. Fraud cases involve painstaking and long-term investigations to reveal the criminals, who are usually organized groups or individuals hiding behind false identifications. Special agents working for forgery squads often have cases referred to them from banks or local police departments that have discovered incidents of forgery.

REQUIREMENTS

High School

You can help prepare for a career as a special agent by doing well in high school. You may receive special consideration by the Secret Service if you have computer training, which is needed to investigate computer fraud, or if you can speak a foreign language, which is useful during investigations and while protecting visiting heads of state or U.S. officials who are working abroad. Specialized skills in electronics, forensics, and other investigative areas are highly regarded. Aside from school, doing something unique and positive for your city or neighborhood, or becoming involved in community organizations can improve your chances of being selected by the Secret Service.

Postsecondary Training

The Secret Service recruits special agents at the GS-5 and GS-7 grade levels. You can qualify at the GS-5 level in one of three ways: obtain a four-year degree from an accredited college or university; work for at least three years in a criminal investigative or law enforcement field and gain knowledge and experience in applying laws relating to criminal violations; or obtain an equivalent combination of education and experience. You can qualify at the GS-7 level by achieving superior academic scores (defined as a grade point average of at least 2.95 on a 4.0 scale), going to graduate school and studying a directly related field, or gaining an additional year of criminal investigative experience.

All newly hired special agents go through nine weeks of training at the Federal Law Enforcement Training Center in Glynco, Georgia, and then 11 weeks of specialized training at the Secret Service's Training Academy in Beltsville, Maryland. During training, new agents take comprehensive courses in protective techniques, criminal and constitutional law, criminal investigative procedures, use of scientific investigative devices, first aid, the use of firearms, and defensive measures. Special agents also learn about collecting evidence, surveillance techniques, undercover operation, and courtroom demeanor. Specialized training includes skills such as firefighting and protection aboard airplanes. The classroom study is supplemented by on-the-job training, and special agents go through advanced in-service training throughout their careers.

New special agents usually begin work at the field offices where they first applied. Their initial work is investigative in nature and is closely supervised. After about five years, agents are usually transferred to a protection assignment.

Other Requirements

In addition to the educational requirements, special agents must meet the following criteria: Be a U.S. citizen; be at least 21 and less than 37 years of age at the time of appointment; have uncorrected vision no worse than 20/60 in each eye, correctable to 20/20 in each eye; be in excellent health and physical condition; pass the Treasury Enforcement Agent exam; and undergo a complete background investigation, including in-depth interviews, drug screening, medical examination, and polygraph examination.

The Secret Service is looking for smart, upstanding citizens who will give a favorable representation of the U.S. government. The agency looks for people with strong ethics, morals, and virtues, and then they teach them how to be special agents. "You can be a crackerjack lawyer, but have some ethical problems in your background, and we wouldn't hire you as an agent even though we would love to have your expertise," Norm Jarvis says.

Learn More About It

Holden, Henry. *To Be a U.S. Secret Service Agent*. Osceola, Wisc.: Zenith Press, 2006.

Melanson, Philip H. *The Secret Service: The Hidden History of an Enigmatic Agency*. New York: Carroll & Grap, 2005.

National Geographic. *Inside the U.S. Secret Service*. (DVD.) National Geographic Video: 2004.

Petro, Joseph. *Standing Next to History: An Agent's Life Inside the Secret Service*. New York: St. Martin's Griffin, 2006.

Seidman, David. *Secret Service Agents: Life Protecting the President*. New York: Rosen Publishing Group, 2002.

Souter, Gerry. *Secret Service Agent and Careers in Federal Protection*. Berkeley Heights, N.J.: Enslow Publishers, 2006.

Special agents also need dedication, which can be demonstrated through a candidate's grade point average in high school and college. Applicants must have a drug-free background. Even experimental drug use can be a reason to dismiss an applicant from the hiring process. Special agents also need to be confident and honest—with no criminal background. "It's important as a representative of the President's Office that you conduct yourself well, that you look good, and that you're able to command some respect," Jarvis says. "Anything even as minor as shoplifting is an indicator of a personality problem."

Since special agents must travel for their jobs—Jarvis spends about 30 percent of his time on the road—interested applicants should be flexible and willing to be away from home. Jarvis says the traveling is one of the downfalls of the job, often requiring him to leave his wife and two children at a moment's notice.

EXPLORING

The Secret Service offers the Stay-In-School Program for high school students. The program allows students who meet financial eligibility guidelines to earn money and some benefits by working part time, usually in a clerical job, for the agency. There are many requirements and application guidelines for this program, so contact the Secret Service's Stay-In-School office at the address given at the end of this article.

The Secret Service also offers the Cooperative Education Program as a way for the agency to identify and train highly motivated students for careers as special agents. Participants in this paid program learn more about the Secret Service and gain on-the-job training, with the possibility of working full time for the Secret Service upon graduation. The two-year work-study program includes classroom training and hands-on training that will prepare students for the following Secret Service careers: accountant, budget analyst, computer specialist, computer research specialist, electronic engineer, intelligence research specialist, management specialist, personnel management specialist, telecommunications specialist, and visual information specialist. Students working toward a bachelor's degree must complete 1,040 hours of study-related work requirements.

To be considered for the program, you must be enrolled full time in an accredited educational program; be enrolled in your school's cooperative education program; maintain a 3.0 grade point average in either undergraduate or graduate studies; be a U.S. citizen; be enrolled in a field of study related to the position you are applying for; pass a drug test; and pass a preliminary background investigation and possibly a polygraph test. Male applicants born after

December 31, 1959, must be registered with the Selective Service System or be legally exempt from doing so. Further, your school must sign a working agreement with the Secret Service.

There is also a Cooperative Education Program for criminal investigators (special agents), which, in addition to the general requirements stated above, requires that participants be enrolled in a graduate or law degree program and pass polygraph and medical examinations. This two-year program, available only in the Washington, D.C., area, provides rudimentary training for the special agent position, introducing participants to the investigative and protective techniques that agents use.

Students in the Cooperative Education Program work part time, which is between 16 and 32 hours a week. They may work full time during holidays and school breaks. They receive some federal benefits including a retirement plan, life and health insurance, annual and sick leave, holiday pay, awards, and promotions.

You must submit a variety of forms to apply for this program, so contact the Secret Service's Cooperative Education coordinator at the address given at the end of the article for more information. In addition, you may be able to apply for the program through the cooperative education program at your school.

STARTING OUT

Norm Jarvis didn't set out to become a special agent. As a teenager, he admired a neighbor who worked as a deputy sheriff. As Jarvis grew older and had to make decisions about college and work, he realized he wanted to go into law enforcement. At the age of 18, he volunteered to go into the U.S. Army to train with the military police. When Jarvis left the service, he used his veteran's benefits to help him get a bachelor's degree in psychology from Westminster College. "I have an innate interest in why people do the things they do," he says. Norm also earned a master's degree in public administration from Utah University. He spent eight years working as a police officer before he decided to apply to the Secret Service. He wasn't satisfied with his police officer's salary and was tired of the "day-to-day emotional trauma of being an officer." Jarvis loved to travel and was impressed by some special agents he had met, so he decided that becoming a special agent would be a way for him to progress professionally and work in an exciting position.

The Secret Service warns that because they have many well-qualified applicants and few anticipated vacancies, the chance that you will be hired is limited. On top of that, the hiring process can take up to a year or more because of the thoroughness of the selection process.

If you are ready to apply for a special agent job, make sure you meet the requirements described above, then submit a typewritten Standard Form 171, Application for Federal Employment. If you have graduated from college, you will also need to submit an official transcript. Alternatively, you can submit an Optional Application for Federal Employment or a resume, but you will have to complete some accompanying forms, so be sure to check with the Secret Service field office nearest you before doing so to find out exactly what forms to fill out. The field office in your area should be listed in the government section of your telephone book.

The Secret Service only accepts applications for current job openings. To find out what vacancies currently exist, use the contact information at the end of this article.

ADVANCEMENT

Norm Jarvis began working in the Secret Service's Salt Lake City field office in 1984. He was transferred to the Organized Crime Task Force in the Washington, D.C., field office in 1987. In 1990, Jarvis was promoted to the position of instructor at the Office of Training, and he was transferred to the Presidential Protective Division in 1994. Jarvis went to Montana in 1997, after being promoted to the position of resident agent of the Great Falls field office. Currently, he is a special agent once again in the Salt Lake City office.

Generally, special agents begin their careers by spending five to 10 years performing primarily investigative duties at a field office. Then, they are usually assigned to a protective assignment for three to five years. After 12 or 13 years, special agents become eligible to move into supervisory positions. A typical promotion path moves special agents to the position of senior agent, then resident agent in charge of a district, assistant to the special agent in charge, and, finally, special agent in charge of a field office or headquarters division. Promotion is awarded based upon performance, and since the Secret Service employs many highly skilled professionals, competition for promotion is strong.

Special agents can retire after 20 years and after they reach the age of 50. Special agents must retire before the age of 57, though. Jarvis plans to continue working with the Secret Service until retirement. When he does retire, Jarvis does not plan on pursuing law enforcement activities. Instead, he would like to earn a doctorate in psychology, sociology, or criminology and teach at the college level.

Some retired agents are hired by corporations to organize the logistics of getting either people or products from one place to another. Others work as bodyguards, private investigators, security consultants, and local law enforcement officials.

EARNINGS

Special agents generally receive law enforcement availability pay (LEAP) on top of their base pay. Agents usually start at the GS-5 or GS-7 grade levels, which in 2006 were $25,195 and $31,209, respectively, excluding LEAP. (Salaries may be slightly higher in some areas with high costs of living.) Agents automatically advance by two pay grades each year until they reach the GS-12 level, which, in 2006, was $55,360, excluding LEAP. Agents must compete for positions above the GS-12 level; however, the majority of agents reach GS-13—$65,832, excluding LEAP, in 2006—in the course of their careers. Top officials in the Secret Service are appointed to Senior Executive Service (SES) positions; they do not receive the availability pay. Top SES salaries are well over $150,000 a year.

Benefits for special agents include low-cost health and life insurance, annual and sick leave, paid holidays, and a comprehensive retirement program. In addition, free financial protection is provided to agents and their families in the event of job-related injury or death.

WORK ENVIRONMENT

A Secret Service special agent is assigned to a field office or one of three Washington, D.C., divisions. Agents on investigative assignments may spend much time doing research with the office as base, or they may be out in the field, doing undercover or surveillance work. Protective and investigative assignments can keep a special agent away from home for long periods of time, depending on the situation. Preparations for the president's visits to cities in the United States generally take no more than a week. However, a large event attracting foreign dignitaries, such as the Asian Pacific Conference in the state of Washington, can take months to plan. Special agents at field offices assigned to investigate crimes are called out regularly to serve temporary protective missions. During presidential campaign years, agents typically serve three-week protective assignments, work three weeks back at their field offices, and then start the process over again. Special agents always work at least 40 hours a week and often work a minimum of 50 hours each week.

One of the drawbacks of being a special agent is the potential danger involved. A special agent was shot in the stomach in 1981, during an assassination attempt on President Ronald Reagan. Other agents have been killed on the job in helicopter accidents, surveillance assignments, and protective operations, to name a few.

For most agents, however, the benefits outweigh the drawbacks. For Norm Jarvis, the excitement and profound importance of his work give him great job satisfaction. "There are times when you are involved in world history and you witness history being made, or you are present when historical decisions are being made, and you feel privileged to be a part of making history, albeit you're behind the scenes and never recognized for it," he says. However, according to one of Jarvis's coworkers, the job is not always glamorous and can be "like going out in your backyard in your best suit and standing for three hours."

OUTLOOK

Compared to other federal law enforcement agencies, the Secret Service is small. The agency focuses on its protective missions and is not interested in expanding its responsibilities. "We want to be the best at protection, and I think we are the best in the world and that suits us fine," Norm Jarvis says. As a result, the Secret Service will likely not grow much, unless the president and Congress decide to expand the agency's duties.

In spite of increased high-alert conditions as a result of terrorist threats, the Secret Service still employs a small number of people, and their new hires each year are limited. Officials anticipate that the job availability could increase slightly over the next few years.

FOR MORE INFORMATION

Your local Secret Service field office or headquarters office can provide more information on becoming a special agent. To learn about careers, download employment applications, and read frequently asked questions, check out the following Web site:

U.S. Secret Service
245 Murray Drive, Building 410
Washington, DC 20223-0007
Tel: 202-406-5800
http://www.secretservice.gov

Security Consultants and Guards

OVERVIEW

Security consultants and *security guards* are responsible for protecting public and private property against theft, fire, vandalism, illegal entry, and acts of violence. They may work for commercial or government organizations or private individuals. More than one million security workers are employed in the United States.

HISTORY

People have been concerned with protecting valuable possessions since they began accumulating goods. At first, most security plans were rather simple. In earliest times, members of extended families or several families would band together to watch food, clothing, livestock, and other valuables. As personal wealth grew, the wealthier members of a society would often assign some of their servants to protect their property and families from theft and violence. Soldiers often filled this function as well. During the Middle Ages, many towns and villages hired guards to patrol the streets at night as protection against fire, theft, and hostile intrusion. Night watchmen continued to play an important role in the security of many towns and cities until well into the 19th century.

The first public police forces were organized in about the middle of the 19th century. These were largely limited to cities, however, and the need for protection and safety of goods and property led many to

QUICK FACTS

School subjects
Business
Psychology

Personal Skills
Communication/ideas
Mechanical/manipulative

Work Environment
Indoors and outdoors
One location with some travel

Minimum Education Level
Bachelor's degree (security consultants)
High school diploma (security guards)

Salary Range
$14,550 to $20,760 to $34,470+

Certification or Licensing
Recommended

Outlook
As fast as the average

DOT
189

GOE
04.03.03

NOC
6651

O*NET-SOC
33-9032.00

A security guard stands at his post in front of the Washington Monument. *(Guy Crittenden/Index Stock Imagery)*

supplement police forces with private security forces. In the United States, ranchers and others hired armed guards to protect their property. Soon, people began to specialize in offering comprehensive security and detective services. Allan Pinkerton was one of the first such security agents. In 1861, Pinkerton was hired to guard President-elect Abraham Lincoln on his way to his inauguration.

As police forces at local, state, and federal levels were established across the country, night watchmen and other security personnel continued to play an important role in protecting the goods and property of private businesses. The growth of industry created a need for people to patrol factories and warehouses. Many companies hired private security forces to guard factories during strikes. Banks, department stores, and museums employed security guards to guard against theft and vandalism. Other security personnel began to specialize in designing security systems—with considerations including the types of safes and alarms to be used and the stationing of security guards—to protect both public and private facilities. Government and public facilities, such as ammunition dumps, nuclear power facilities, dams, and oil pipelines, also needed security systems and guards to protect them.

Security systems have grown increasingly sophisticated with the introduction of technologies such as cameras, closed-circuit television, video, and computers. The security guard continues to play an important role in the protection of people and property. The increasing use of computers has aided the guard or security technician by protecting electronic data and transmissions. The increasing number of terrorist threats has also led to the more frequent use of security services.

THE JOB

A security consultant is engaged in protective service work. Anywhere that valuable property or information is present or people are at risk, a security consultant may be called in to devise and implement security plans that offer protection. Security consultants may work for a variety of clients, including large stores, art museums, factories, laboratories, data processing centers, and political candidates. They are involved in preventing theft, vandalism, fraud, kidnapping, and other crimes. Specific job responsibilities depend on the type and size of the client's company and the scope of the security system required.

Security consultants always work closely with company officials or other appropriate individuals in the development of a comprehensive security program that will fit the needs of individual clients. After discussing goals and objectives with the relevant company executives, consultants study and analyze the physical conditions and internal operations of a client's operation. They learn much by simply observing day-to-day operations.

The size of the security budget also influences the type of equipment ordered and methods used. For example, a large factory that produces military hardware may fence off its property and place electric eyes around the perimeter of the fence. They may also install perimeter alarms and use passkeys to limit access to restricted areas. A smaller company may use only entry-control mechanisms in specified areas. The consultant may recommend sophisticated technology, such as closed-circuit surveillance or ultrasonic motion detectors, alone or in addition to security personnel. Usually, a combination of electronic and human resources is used.

Security consultants not only devise plans to protect equipment but also recommend procedures on safeguarding and possibly destroying classified material. Increasingly, consultants are being called on to develop strategies to safeguard data processing equipment. They may have to develop measures to safeguard transmission lines against unwanted or unauthorized interceptions.

Once a security plan has been developed, the consultant oversees the installation of the equipment, ensures that it is working properly, and checks frequently with the client to ensure that the client is satisfied. In the case of a crime against the facility, a consultant investigates the nature of the crime (often in conjunction with police or other investigators) and then modifies the security system to safeguard against similar crimes in the future.

Many consultants work for security firms that have several types of clients, such as manufacturing and telecommunications plants and facilities. Consultants may handle a variety of clients or work exclusively in a particular area. For example, one security consultant may be assigned to handle the protection of nuclear power plants and another to handle data processing companies.

Security consultants may be called on to safeguard famous individuals or persons in certain positions from kidnapping or other type of harm. They provide security services to officers of large companies, media personalities, and others who want their safety and privacy protected. These consultants, like bodyguards, plan and review client travel itineraries and usually accompany the client on trips, checking accommodations and appointment locations along the way. They often check the backgrounds of people who will interact with the client, especially those who see the client infrequently.

Security consultants are sometimes called in for special events, such as sporting events and political rallies, when there is no specific fear of danger but rather a need for overall coordination of a large security operation. The consultants oversee security preparation—such as the stationing of appropriate personnel at all points of entry and exit—and then direct specific responses to any security problems.

Security officers develop and implement security plans for companies that manufacture or process material for the federal government. They ensure that their clients' security policies comply with federal regulations in such categories as the storing and handling of classified documents and restricting access to authorized personnel only.

Security guards have various titles, depending on the type of work they do and the setting in which they work. They may be referred to as *patrollers* (who are assigned to cover a certain area), *bouncers* (who eject unruly people from places of entertainment), *golf-course rangers* (who patrol golf courses), or *gate tenders* (who work at security checkpoints).

Many security guards are employed during normal working hours in public and commercial buildings and other areas with a good deal of pedestrian traffic and public contact. Others patrol buildings and grounds outside normal working hours, such as at night and on weekends. Guards usually wear uniforms and may carry a nightstick. Guards who work in situations where they may be called upon to apprehend criminal intruders are usually armed. They may also carry a flashlight, a whistle, a two-way radio, and a watch clock, which is used to record the time at which they reach various checkpoints.

Guards in public buildings may be assigned to a certain post or they may patrol an area. In museums, art galleries, and other public buildings, guards answer visitors' questions and give them directions; they also enforce rules against smoking, touching art objects, and so forth. In commercial buildings, guards may sign people in and out after hours and inspect packages being carried out of the building. Bank guards observe customers carefully for any sign of suspicious behavior that may signal a possible robbery attempt. In department stores, security guards often work with undercover detectives to watch for theft by customers or store employees. Guards at large public gatherings such as sporting events and conventions keep traffic moving, direct people to their seats, and eject unruly spectators. Guards employed at airports limit access to boarding areas to passengers only. They make sure people entering passenger areas have valid tickets and observe passengers and their baggage as they pass through X-ray machines and metal detection equipment.

After-hours guards are usually employed at industrial plants, defense installations, construction sites, and transport facilities such as docks and railroad yards. They make regular rounds on foot or, if the premises are very large, in motorized vehicles. They check to be sure that no unauthorized persons are on the premises, that doors and windows are secure, and that no property is missing. They may be equipped with walkie-talkies to report in at intervals to a central guard station. Sometimes guards perform custodial duties, such as turning on lights and setting thermostats.

In a large organization, a *security officer* is often in charge of the guard force; in a small organization, a single worker may be responsible for all security measures. As more businesses purchase advanced electronic security systems to protect their properties, more guards are being assigned to stations where they monitor perimeter security, environmental functions, communications, and other systems. In many cases, these guards maintain radio contact with other guards patrolling on foot or in motor vehicles. Some guards use computers to store information on matters relevant to security such as visitors or suspicious occurrences during their time on duty.

Security guards work for government agencies or for private companies hired by government agencies. Their task is usually to guard secret or restricted installations domestically or in foreign countries. They spend much of their time patrolling areas, which they may do on foot, on horseback, or in automobiles or aircraft. They may monitor activities in an area through the use of surveillance cameras and video screens. Their assignments usually include detecting and preventing unauthorized activities, searching for explosive devices, standing watch during secret and hazardous experiments, and performing other routine police duties within government installations.

Security guards are usually armed and may be required to use their weapons or other kinds of physical force to prevent some kinds of activities. They are usually not, however, required to remove explosive devices from an installation. When they find such devices, they notify a bomb disposal unit, which is responsible for removing and then defusing or detonating the device.

REQUIREMENTS

High School

A high school diploma is preferred for security guards and required for security consultants, who should also go on to obtain a college degree. Security guards must be high school graduates. In addition, they should expect to receive from three to six months of specialized training in security procedures and technology. If you would like to be a security guard, you should take mathematics courses while in high school to ensure that you can perform basic arithmetic operations with different units of measure; compute ratios, rates, and percentages; and interpret charts and graphs.

You should take English courses to develop your reading and writing skills. You should be able to read manuals, memos, textbooks, and other instructional materials and write reports with correct spelling, grammar, and punctuation. You should also be able to speak to small groups with poise and confidence.

Postsecondary Training

Most companies prefer to hire security consultants who have at least a college degree. An undergraduate or associate's degree in criminal justice, business administration, or related field is best. Course work should be broad and include business management, communications, computer courses, sociology, and statistics. As the security consulting field becomes more competitive, many consultants choose to get a master's in business administration (MBA) or other graduate degree.

Although there are no specific educational or professional requirements, many security guards have had previous experience with police work or other forms of crime prevention. It is helpful if a person develops an expertise in a specific area. For example, if you want to work devising plans securing data processing equipment, it is helpful to have previous experience working with computers.

Certification or Licensing

Many security consultants are certified by the Certified Protection Professionals. To be eligible for certification, a consultant must pass a written test and have 10 years' work and educational experience in the security profession. Information on certification is available from the American Society for Industrial Security, a professional organization to which many security consultants belong.

Virtually every state has licensing or registration requirements for security guards who work for contract security agencies. Registration generally requires that a person newly hired as a guard be reported to the licensing authorities, usually the state police department or special state licensing commission. To be granted a license, individuals generally must be 18 years of age, have no convictions for perjury or acts of violence, pass a background investigation, and complete classroom training on a variety of subjects, including property rights, emergency procedures, and capture of suspected criminals.

Other Requirements

For security guards, general good health (especially vision and hearing), alertness, emotional stability, and the ability to follow directions are important characteristics. Military service and experience in local or state police departments are assets. Prospective guards should have clean police records. Some employers require applicants to take a polygraph examination or a written test that indicates honesty, attitudes, and other personal qualities. Most employers require applicants and experienced workers to submit to drug screening tests as a condition of employment.

For some hazardous or physically demanding jobs, guards must be under a certain age and meet height and weight standards. For top-level security positions in facilities such as nuclear power plants or vulnerable information centers, guards may be required to complete a special training course. They may also need to fulfill certain relevant academic requirements.

Guards employed by the federal government must be U.S. armed forces veterans, have some previous experience as guards, and pass a written examination. Many positions require experience with firearms. In many situations, guards must be bonded.

Security technicians need good eyesight and should be in good physical shape, able to lift at least 50 pounds, climb ladders, stairs, poles, and ropes, and maintain their balance on narrow, slippery, or moving surfaces. They should be able to stoop, crawl, crouch, and kneel with ease.

EXPLORING

Part-time or summer employment as a clerk with a security firm is an excellent way to gain insight into the skills and temperament needed to become a security consultant. Discussions with professional security consultants are another way of exploring career opportunities in this field. You may find it helpful to join a safety patrol at school.

If you are interested in a particular area of security consulting, such as data processing, for example, you can join a club or association to learn more about the field. This is a good way to make professional contacts.

Opportunities for part-time or summer work as security guards are not generally available to high school students. You may, however, work as a lifeguard, on a safety patrol, and as a school hallway monitor, which can provide helpful experience.

EMPLOYERS

Security services is one of the largest employment fields in the United States. Over one million persons are employed in the security industry in the United States. Industrial security firms and guard agencies, also called contract security firms, employ over half of all guards, while the remainder are in-house guards employed by various establishments.

STARTING OUT

People interested in careers in security services generally apply directly to security companies. Some jobs may be available through state or private employment services. People interested in security technician positions should apply directly to government agencies.

Beginning security personnel receive varied amounts of training. Training requirements are generally increasing as modern, highly sophisticated security systems become more common. Many employers give newly hired security guards instruction before they start the job and also provide several weeks of on-the-job training. Guards receive training in protection, public relations, report writing, crisis deterrence, first aid, and drug control.

Those employed at establishments that place a heavy emphasis on security usually receive extensive formal training. For example, guards at nuclear power plants may undergo several months of training before being placed on duty under close supervision. Guards may be taught to use firearms, administer first aid, operate alarm systems and electronic security equipment, handle emergencies, and spot and deal with security problems.

Older people who are retired police officers or armed forces veterans fill many of the less strenuous guard positions. Because of the odd hours required for many positions, this occupation appeals to many people seeking part-time work or second jobs.

Most entry-level positions for security consultants are filled by those with a bachelor's or associate's degree in criminal justice, business administration, or a related field. Those with a high school diploma and some experience in the field may find work with a security consulting firm, although they usually begin as security guards and become consultants only after further training.

Because many consulting firms have their own techniques and procedures, most require entry-level personnel to complete an on-the-job training program, during the course of which they learn company policies.

ADVANCEMENT

In most cases, security guards receive periodic salary increases, and guards employed by larger security companies or as part of a military-style guard force may increase their responsibilities or move up in rank. A guard with outstanding ability, especially with some college education, may move up to the position of chief guard, gaining responsibility for the supervision and training of an entire guard force in an industrial plant or a department store, or become director of security services for a business or commercial building. A few guards with management skills open their own contract security guard agencies; other guards become licensed private detectives. Experienced guards may become bodyguards for political figures, executives, and celebrities, or choose to enter a police department or other law enforcement agency. Additional training may lead to a career as a corrections officer.

Increased training and experience with a variety of security and surveillance systems may lead security guards into higher paying security consultant careers. Security consultants with experience may advance to management positions or they may start their own private consulting firms. Instruction and training of security personnel is another advancement opportunity for security guards, consultants, and technicians.

EARNINGS

Earnings for security consultants vary greatly depending on the consultant's training and experience. Entry-level consultants with bachelor's degrees commonly start at $26,000 to $32,000 per year. Consultants with graduate degrees begin at $34,000 to $41,000 per year, and experienced consultants may earn $50,000 to $100,000 per year or more. Many consultants work on a per-project basis, with rates of up to $75 per hour.

Average starting salaries for security guards and technicians vary according to their level of training and experience, and the location where they work. Median annual earnings for security guards were $20,760 in 2005, according to the U.S. Department of Labor. Experienced security guards earned more than $34,470 per year in 2005, while the least experienced security guards earned less than $14,550 annually. Entry-level guards working for contract agencies may receive little more than the minimum wage. In-house guards generally earn higher wages and have greater job security and better advancement potential.

WORK ENVIRONMENT

Consultants usually divide their time between their offices and a client's business. Much time is spent analyzing various security apparatuses and developing security proposals. The consultant talks with a variety of employees at a client's company, including the top officials, and discusses alternatives with other people at the consulting firm. A consultant makes a security proposal presentation to the client and then works with the client on any modifications. Consultants must be sensitive to budget issues and develop security systems that their clients can afford.

Consultants may specialize in one type of security work (nuclear power plants, for example) or work for a variety of large and small clients, such as museums, data processing companies, and banks. Although there may be a lot of travel and some work may require outdoor activity, there will most likely be no strenuous work. A consultant may oversee the implementation of a large security system but is not involved in the actual installation process. A consultant may have to confront suspicious people but is not expected to do the work of a police officer.

Security guards and technicians may work indoors or outdoors. In high-crime areas and industries vulnerable to theft and vandalism, there may be considerable physical danger. Guards who work in museums, department stores, and other buildings and facilities remain on their feet for long periods of time, either standing still or walking while on patrol. Guards assigned to reception areas or security control rooms may remain at their desks for the entire shift. Much of their work is routine and may be tedious at times, yet guards must remain constantly alert during their shift. Guards who work with the public, especially at sporting events and concerts, may have to confront unruly and sometimes hostile people. Bouncers often confront intoxicated people and are frequently called upon to intervene in physical altercations.

Many companies employ guards around the clock in three shifts, including weekends and holidays, and assign workers to these shifts on a rotating basis. The same is true for security technicians guarding government facilities and installations. Those with less seniority will likely have the most erratic schedules. Many guards work alone for an entire shift, usually lasting eight hours. Lunches and other meals are often taken on the job, so that constant vigilance is maintained.

OUTLOOK

Employment for guards and other security personnel is expected to increase as fast as the average career through 2014, as crime rates rise with the overall population growth. Public concern about crime, vandalism, and terrorism continues to increase. Many job openings will be created as a result of the high turnover of workers in this field.

A factor adding to this demand is the trend for private security firms to perform duties previously handled by police officers, such as courtroom security. Private security companies employ security technicians to guard many government sites, such as nuclear testing facilities. Private companies also operate many training facilities for government security technicians and guards, as well as providing police services for some communities.

FOR MORE INFORMATION

For information on educational programs and certification procedures, contact
American Society for Industrial Security
1625 Prince Street
Alexandria, VA 22314-2818
Tel: 703-519-6200
Email: asis@asisonline.org
http://www.asisonline.org

For information on union membership, contact
Security, Police, and Fire Professionals of America
25510 Kelly Road
Roseville, MI 40866-4932
Tel: 800-228-7492
http://www.spfpa.org

Index